The Beggar's Opera
by Mr. Gay

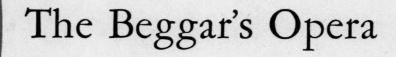

The Beggar's Opera

by John Gay

TO WHICH IS ADDED
THE MUSIC TO EACH SONG

with an introduction by A. P. Herbert
and illustrations by Mariette Lydis

THE HERITAGE PRESS
New York

Preface

THE BEGGAR'S OPERA was first performed in 1728, and ran for sixty-two nights. Nearly two hundred years later it was presented by Sir Nigel Playfair at the Lyric Theatre, Hammersmith: and it ran for three and a half years (June 5, 1920 to December 17, 1923).

Its success was not immediate; and when it came it seemed fantastic. The wise men of the "West End" laughed at the continual throngs clamouring for encores, at the individuals who boasted their eighty and more attendances. But all this happened. It became impossible to think of the little Lyric without "the Beggar." He became a part of the furniture of Hammersmith. Lovat Fraser's simple but inspired set seemed as solid as the Town Hall. Frederick Ranalow as Macheath was an institution, and even a change in Jenny Diver's department provoked much talk in the town. In thousands of homes all over England, Frederick Austin's ingenious and delicate score was a permanent ornament of the piano and restored the lost habit of family singing. And now the little daughter of Arnold Pilbeam, the one and only Beggar, Miss Nova Pilbeam, is a grown-up star. Sir Nigel Playfair and Lovat Fraser are dead, and all this seems very far away. But Gay's work lives on. There have been queer twisted versions of it in German and in French. We may make due allowance for the wizardry of Sir Nigel and his gallant band, for the freaks of fashion and the charm of music, but beyond that, what is the secret power of this piece that it endures so obstinately?

Satire, to be effective, must be good entertainment as well: as a parody should carry interest to the reader who knows nothing of the model. And what happens in this queer world is that the point of the satire is forgotten and the entertainment survives. This is a good thing, for it confirms the view that politics are ephemeral, but art endures. The generations which applaud *H.M.S. Pinafore* and *Patience* and *Iolanthe* to-day are many leagues remote, not only from the "topical allusions," but from the very foundations of those admirable works, but it does not matter. So with *The Beggar's Opera*. When I first saw it I understood dimly what the Encyclopaedia tells us, that Gay in this piece was "caricaturing Sir Robert Walpole." But was Sir Robert "Macheath," "Peachum," or who? And why? I did not know then. I do not know now. It did not, and does not, seem to matter much. The play is full of general digs at the rich and great: but every light lyrical piece has been full of them since the time of Aristophanes, and I dare say earlier than that. No, if we must go behind the entertainment and look for solids, what interests me is not the political satire but the social picture: and what attracts, I think, is the humanity behind the picture, though that may seem a strange assertion to many who think of the opera as coarse and brutal.

Any future historian who goes for evidence to our contemporary musical plays will form a most erroneous impression of our time. He will see a world in which there is neither work nor unemployment; where the young women spend most of their lives in bathing-dresses or expensive evening frocks, at race-courses and cabarets, in enormous liners and vast milliners' shops; everybody is very well-dressed and has nothing much to do; there are neither politics nor social problems; love and courting are the only things that matter; and the sole cloud upon the blissful scene is the temporary estrangement of Boy and Girl.

But the social picture in *The Beggar's Opera* is true. Truth may be fantasticated in a musical play: but this is rather a restrained piece of reporting. And I do not say that without foundation. In 1914, as I bicycled from Bethnal Green to join the Great War at Lambeth, I stopped at an old book-shop in the Minories, and there I picked up a complete set of the *Proceedings of London Sessions from December, 1732, to October, 1733: bound up with the Accounts of the Ordinary of Newgate of the Behaviour, Confession, and Dying Words of the Malefactors who were executed at Tyburn* during that period. 1732—and *The Beggar's Opera* was produced in 1728. The Proceedings are reported verbatim, with apparent fidelity and astonishing detail. All the ingredients of the opera are there: the highwayman, the informers, the pickpockets, the hussies, the gin, the same immoral, callous, humorous, fascinating flavour. In the light of these pages Gay's work becomes terribly real, though his tale is almost drab beside the average story of the Proceedings. Not even his style is too ornate: for in those days every common vagabond seems to have had a superb literary name and gave his evidence in vivid prose. Here are a few names picked at random from the trials: Barbara Dewfly, Sarah Laverstitch, Clarety-face Hannah (a hussy, I need hardly say), Jeremiah Scruby, Zacahariah Mines, Thomas Bonnamy, Mr. Tabbery, a Cabinet Maker, Benedict Duddle, Surgeon, Richard Punt, Constable, Sarah Trantum, Brock *(alias* Poplet), Matthew Monger, Martha Negus, Charles Bosantine, Susan Marriage, Michael Roop, Stephen Triquet, Robert Bugbeard, Philadelphia Allen. . . . The informer was the principal bulwark of the law and the Proceedings bristle with Peachums and "thief-takers":—

Mascall made an agreement with Kirk, Brock, Will James, and the rest of the thief-takers in Drury Lane, to apprehend us, and they are to share the Reward among them: Kirk would have taken my life a Week or two before this Affair, and he swore then he would hang me before a Fortnight was at an End.

Court: Kirk has not Appear'd against you.

Welton: He's ashamed to appear now, he's so well known; he was concern'd in taking Charles Patrick and Will Meeds, and appear'd against them to get the Reward. But I told him, he should have no more hundred and forty Pounds, and upon that he swore that I threaten'd to set his House on Fire, and he lent Mascall these Pistols on purpose to produce in Court against us.

A certain "Powers *alias* Cabbage" runs through all the Sessions:—

Two years ago this Cabbage was taken up for exhorting

of Money out of People, and he has been out of Jail but 3 Months, and yet he has got 18 Robberies in his Information: Is it likely he could be concerned in so many Facts, and have so many Accomplices in so short a time? He has put a great many Innocent men, besides me, in his Information. I never drank but twice with him in my life.

Court: Has not the Prisoner been an Evidence himself?

A Turnkey: Yes, my Lord, he was an Evidence last Summer against 5 young fellows, who were all capitally convicted, but were afterwards transported.

And here is "Cabbage" testifying against *Filch:*—

I have known Elms three years. He never robb'd in my Company before, except only trifling Things, as when we took some Goods out of a Sash Window in Chancery Lane. I was with him in the Poultry Compter, where he robb'd two Taylors, and it cost me six Guineas to have the Bill brought in *Ignoramus.* And we have been in Newgate together too.

Kemp (to Powers): Was I ever with you since you have been an Evidence?

Powers: No, I have been in Jail ever since.

Kemp: I mean, before you were an Evidence?

Powers: Yes, when my Lady Page dy'd, he carry'd me down to Greenwich to cut Pockets at the Burying, and we follow'd her to Bunhill Fields.

Samuel Thomas, who murdered his wife, might have inspired Macheath's sad ditties about women:—

As to the particular Fact for which he died, he said that his Wife having been out and lying by the Door very Drunk he endeavoured to bring her into the House, but she was unwilling to go along with him: and that as he struggled to drag her up Stairs, and she opposing him, he believ'd that she received several hurts, but that he in that affair intended no harm to her, and he alledg'd that the Women who appear'd against him were all her Companions, and had no Good Will for him.

And here is an attempt at treachery by Jenny Diver:—

So I found him with his Wife in Lambeth-Marsh, when the Wife having taken the Watch and Money, swore she would hang us both. Carr, hearing her express herself after that manner, beat her very severely.

Here, may be, is Diana Trapes:—

Court: Soams is your Name? How long have you gone by that name?

Isabella Eaton: About a twelve-month.

Court: I think I have tried you here by another Name.

Eaton: Very like you might try me, my Lord, and by another Name too; but what if you did? I was Innocent, and my Jury acquitted me. I never came here for my Crimes, but my Passions. I keep the *Two Blue-Posts,* in the Hay Market.

Mr. James Guthrie, the Ordinary of Newgate, has much to say about the long career of the great highwayman, William Gordon, who may have been the model for Macheath. He was one of the gentlemanly "collectors" who "never maltreated anybody," but rather endeared himself to those he robbed, except to the unfortunate Mr. Peters, from whom he "raised a contribution" a little on this side of Knightsbridge. Mr. Peters, giving evidence, says:—

> Whether it was after I had given him my Watch or before I cannot be certain, but he snatched off my Hat and Wig. I expostulated with him on that Occasion. I told him that it was very unusual for men of his Profession to take such Things, and that it being very cold it might indanger my Health.

But that seems to have been Mr. Gordon's only lapse from the decent customs of his profession. Certainly the style, and the sentiment, of his "farewell letter to his Son" (before hanging) have the true Macheath flavour (if the Ordinary is to be believed):—

> Slip no opportunity of public Prayer, but be ever ready to hear Sermons; and whenever you can be sure of hearing your Duty explained and recommended; so shall you be out of the Road of Temptation, and avoiding the Paths of Sin, remain unacquainted with Shame. . . .

> Honesty is a Rule from which you must not part, either for the sake of attaining Riches or avoiding little Inconveniences; check yourself in the smallest Transgression of this Kind, and think how Fatal this Neglect has been to me.

> Nature a few Months ago took away your Mother; the

Law will this Day deprive you of a Father; you have now no Parent but the Parent of all Things, on whom you ought to rely with Confidence, that his Favour may never forsake you. Unto his gracious Protection I commend you, in these my last Moments, and I pray that he may give you Power, to live according as he hath taught and commanded. Having fulfilled this my last Act of Duty towards you, I bid you an everlasting Adieu.

From Your Affectionate
Though Disconsolate Father
WILLIAM GORDON

Such was the background of Mr. Gay's London—crazy, comical, callous, incredible. If a man stole "from the person" above the value of 1s. he was hanged (and this was the law till 1808). He was hanged for stealing to the value of 5s. from a shop and 40s. from a dwelling-house. If you burgled or put people "in fear" on the highway values were no matter, and the jury could not save you from the cart by writing down the value of your booty—as juries charitably did. Savage laws, unsupported by a police force, depending largely on dishonour among thieves for their enforcement—life a continual battle between the robbers and the robbed—here was a theme sufficient to touch the imagination of a lively writer, if he had never heard of Sir Robert Walpole: and I suspect that Gay was interested in the underworld for its own sake, like Mr. Edgar Wallace and others. And he saw the underworld as underdogs, which suited his mood and grievances against the great. The English have always loved underdogs: the decent theif, the gentleman burglar, the prostitute with a heart of gold are now familiar figures: and it is this rich vein, perhaps, which gave the opera its robust and irrepressible life. Gay, they tell us, was the father of ballad light opera: but, more than that, he was the forerunner of the crook novel and the gangster film. And criminals do not change much, in essentials, from generation to generation. A few years ago I received a queer letter from a gentleman who had just been released, not for the first time, from "stir," where he had served a sentence for obtaining money by a very ingenious trick. He said that in his cell he had read a contraband copy of *Punch* and would like to see more of my work. I sent him a couple of books: and a little later he wrote and said that he had been inspired to try the "writing-game" too. He enclosed a sketch of prison life: it represented a surreptitious dialogue between two prisoners doing "hard" in the prison workroom. I was struck at once by the "Beggarly" flavour of the dialogue. Here again was the theme which Gay played upon almost to the point of tedium—that if there are any honest men the common thief is the most honest, and the villain who holds his head highest is the worst. Polly, you remember, is upbraided by her parents for marrying a highwayman: but it would have been more shocking if she had married a lord. I thought at first that my correspondent must have come upon Gay as well as *Punch* in prison: but, when I met him he assured me that he had never seen Gay's opera.

Here is an extract from his own work:—

SIDE IN STIR

"What's he in for, Bill?"

"Who, Alf? That miserable looking tyke over there? He's only a debtor. Don't know why they put them among good thieves."

"Did you hear who is to be librarian now that 'long firmer' has done his time?"

"Yes, Alf, a rotten manslaughter, drunk in charge of a car, fifteen months second division. The 'old man' always gives them sort the plum jobs; regular thieves like us, the kind that keep these sort of places going, never get a staff job; all we are fit for is sewing these mail-bags."

"Besides, how can he know what kind of books we like? If I don't get an Edgar Wallace next change day I shall complain to the guv'nor."

"Now then, A.2.10., stop talking, get on with those mail-bags."

"Whisper, Alf, or this screw will 'case' us; can't afford to lose any more remissions, I'm due out next month."

"All right, Bill."

"See that little ginger-headed bloke over there?"

"Which one, Alf? Him sewing tabs?"

"Yes. He sat next to me in chapel yesterday, and I said, 'What are you in for mate?' He said, 'Screwing.' That's what they all say; they don't know, the new ones don't, that their offence is printed on the backs of the cards outside their cells. He's in for neglecting his four kids, so I says to him, 'You couldn't screw the lid off a corned beef tin for your kids, never mind the door off a safe'. You should have seen his face!"

"I reckon they ought to segregate those blokes. It ain't right we should be asked to mix with his sort."

"Do you remember that star bloke who used to work in the stores? Him who went out last week?"

"Not so loud, Bill, this screw's got us taped. I know who you mean though; done a 'stretch' for bigamy, didn't he?"

"Yes, that's the one; used to throw the clean washing at us on bathdays, as much as to say, 'here you are, scum'."

"Well, he's back again; saw him waiting to see the guv'-nor this morning. It seems when he was sentenced last time there was another bird he married besides the one he gets his stretch for, so they pinched him as soon as he got out; he's waiting trial again now. If he had not been so high and mighty we might have told him that it is always policy to have them all taken into consideration. Remember that lot you had taken in, Alf, when we fell last time?"

"I thought the Chief Constable would never finish reading them out."

"Do you think this is the House of Commons, A. 2. 10? If you don't stop talking, you're for the guv'nor in the morning. I have just about had enough of you to-day. Get on with that sewing. Shut up."

"Be glad when this screw gets relieved, Bill, he must have

eyes in the back of his head. See who they have put on the boilers?"

"That ex-officer-looking chap, in for the 'black.' It's the best place for him, out of the way in that boiler-house. No one will speak to him anyway."

The language is not so elegant: but in sentiment my friend is not very far from Peachum's opening song:—

> Through all the employments of life
>   Each neighbour abuses his brother;
> Troll and rogue they call husband and wife:
>   All professions be-rogue one another.
> The priest calls the lawyer a cheat,
>   The lawyer be-knaves the divine;
> And the statesman, because he's so great,
>   Thinks his trade as honest as mine.

A. P. HERBERT

A Note Upon the Text

The Beggar's Opera was first printed in 1728. The present text follows that of the edition of 1765, which has been collated with the first.

A List of the Plates

The Beggar   FACING PAGE 5

Peachum   FACING PAGE 12

Mrs. Peachum   FACING PAGE 21

Polly Peachum   FACING PAGE 28

The Conference   FACING PAGE 37

A Dance "à la Ronde" in the French Manner
FACING PAGE 44

Macheath's Gang   FACING PAGE 53

Captain Macheath   FACING PAGE 60

Jenny Diver and Suky Tawdry
FACING PAGE 77

Mrs. Trapes   FACING PAGE 84

Lucy Lockit   FACING PAGE 93

Dance of the Prisoners
FACING PAGE 100

A List of the Characters

MEN	WOMEN
Mr. Peachum.	Mrs. Peachum.
Lockit.	Polly Peachum.
Macheath.	Lucy Lockit.
Filch.	Diana Trapes.
Jemmy Twitcher.	Mrs. Coaxer.
Crook-finger'd Jack.	Dolly Trull.
Wat Dreary.	Mrs. Vixen.
Robin of Bagshot.	Betty Doxy.
Nimming Ned.	Jenny Diver.
Harry Padington.	Mrs. Slammekin.
Matt of the Mint.	Suky Tawdry.
Ben Budge.	Molly Brazen.
Beggar.	
Player.	
Constables, Drawers,	
Turnkey, &c.	

INTRODUCTION

BEGGAR, PLAYER.

Beggar. If Poverty be a Title to Poetry, I am sure No-body can dispute mine. I own myself of the Company of Beggars; and I make one at their Weekly Festivals at St. Giles. I have a small Yearly Salary for my Catches, and am welcome to a Dinner there whenever I please, which is more than most Poets can say.

Player. As we live by the Muses, 'tis but Gratitude in us to encourage Poetical Merit where-ever we find it. The Muses, contrary to all other Ladies, pay no Distinction to Dress, and never partially mistake the Pertness of Embroidery for Wit, nor the Modesty of Want for Dulness. Be the Author who he will, we push his Play as far as it will go. So (though you are in Want) I wish you Success heartily.

Beggar.   This Piece I own was originally writ for the celebrating the Marriage of James Chanter and Moll Lay, two most excellent Ballad-Singers. I have introduc'd the Similes that are in all your celebrated Operas: The Swallow, the Moth, the Bee, the Ship, the Flower, &c. Besides, I have a Prison Scene which the Ladies always reckon charmingly pathetick. As to the Parts, I have observ'd such a nice Impartiality to our two Ladies, that it is impossible for either of them to take Offence. I hope I may be forgiven, that I have not made my Opera throughout unnatural, like those in vogue; for I have no Recitative: Excepting this, as I have consented to have neither Prologue nor Epilogue, it must be allow'd an Opera in all its forms. The Piece indeed hath been heretofore frequently represented by our selves in our great Room at St. Giles's, so that I cannot too often acknowledge your Charity in bringing it now on the Stage.

Player.   But I see 'tis time for us to withdraw; the Actors are preparing to begin. Play away the Overture.   [*Exeunt.*

Act I Scene I

PEACHUM'S *House*

PEACHUM *sitting at a Table with a large Book of Accounts before him.*

AIR I. AN OLD WOMAN CLOATHED IN GRAY, &c.

Through all the Employments of Life
  Each Neighbour abuses his Brother;
Whore and Rogue they call Husband and Wife:
  All Professions be-rogue one another.

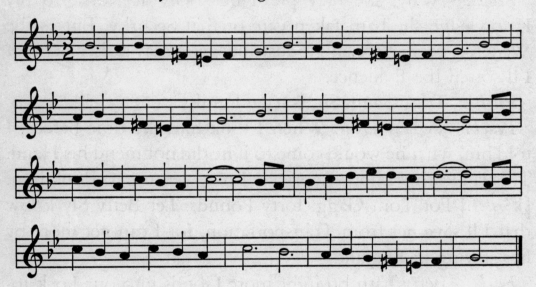

The Priest calls the Lawyer a Cheat,
  The Lawyer be-knaves the Divine;
And the Statesman, because he's so great,
  Thinks his Trade as honest as mine.

A Lawyer is an honest Employment, so is mine. Like me too he acts in a double Capacity, both against Rogues and for 'em; for 'tis but fitting that we should protect and encourage Cheats, since we live by them.

SCENE II

PEACHUM, FILCH.

Filch. Sir, Black Moll hath sent word her Tryal comes on in the Afternoon, and she hopes you will order Matters so as to bring her off.

Peach. Why, she may plead her Belly at worst; to my Knowledge she hath taken care of that Security. But as the Wench is very active and industrious, you may satisfy her that I'll soften the Evidence.

Filch. Tom Gagg, Sir, is found guilty.

Peach. A lazy Dog! When I took him the time before, I told him what he would come to if he did not mend his Hand. This is Death without Reprieve. I may venture to Book him. [*Writes.*] For Tom Gagg, forty Pounds. Let Betty Sly know that I'll save her from Transportation, for I can get more by her staying in England.

Filch. Betty hath brought more Goods into our Lock to-year than any five of the Gang; and in truth, 'tis a pity to lose so good a Customer.

Peach. If none of the Gang take her off, she may, in the common course of Business, live a Twelve-month longer. I

The
Beggar

love to let Women scape. A good Sportsman always lets the Hen Partridges fly, because the breed of the Game depends upon them. Besides, here the Law allows us no Reward; there is nothing to be got by the Death of Women—except our Wives.

Filch. Without dispute, she is a fine Woman! 'Twas to her I was oblig'd for my Education, and (to say a bold Word) she hath train'd up more young Fellows to the Business than the Gaming-table.

Peach. Truly, Filch, thy Observation is right. We and the Surgeons are more beholden to Women than all the Professions besides.

AIR II. THE BONNY GREY-EY'D MORN, &c.

FILCH. *'Tis Woman that seduces all Mankind,*
By her we first were taught the wheedling Arts:

Her very Eyes can cheat; when most she's kind,
She tricks us of our Money with our Hearts.
For her, like Wolves by night we roam for Prey,
And practise ev'ry Fraud to bribe her Charms;
For Suits of Love, like Law, are won by Pay,
And Beauty must be fee'd into our Arms.

Peach. But make haste to Newgate, Boy, and let my Friends know what I intend; for I love to make them easy one way or other.

Filch. When a Gentleman is long kept in suspence, Penitence may break his Spirit ever after. Besides, Certainty gives a Man a good Air upon his Tryal, and makes him risque another without Fear or Scruple. But I'll away, for 'tis a Pleasure to be the Messenger of Comfort to Friends in Affliction.

SCENE III

PEACHUM.

But 'tis now high time to look about me for a decent Execution against next Sessions. I hate a lazy Rogue, by whom one can get nothing 'til he is hang'd. A Register of the Gang, [*Reading.*] Crooked-finger'd Jack. A Year and a half in the Service; Let me see how much the Stock owes to his Industry; one, two, three, four, five Gold Watches, and seven Silver ones. A mighty clean-handed Fellow! Sixteen Snuff-boxes, five of them of true Gold. Six dozen of Handkerchiefs, four silver-hilted Swords, half a dozen of Shirts, three Tye-Perriwigs, and a Piece of Broad Cloth. Considering these are only the Fruits of his leisure Hours, I don't know a prettier Fellow, for no Man alive hath a more engaging Presence of Mind upon the Road. Wat Dreary, alias Brown Will, an irregular Dog, who hath an underhand way of disposing of his Goods. I'll try him only for a Sessions or two longer upon his good Behaviour. Harry Padington, a poor petty-larceny Rascal, without the least Genius; that Fellow, though he were to live these six Months, will never come to the Gallows with any Credit. Slippery Sam; he goes off the next Sessions, for the Villain hath the Impudence to have views of following his Trade as a Taylor, which he calls an honest Employment. Matt of the Mint; listed not above a Month ago, a promising sturdy Fellow, and diligent in his way; somewhat too bold and hasty, and may raise good Contributions on the Publick, if he does not cut himself short by Murder. Tom Tipple, a guzzling, soaking Sot, who is always too drunk to stand himself, or to make others stand. A Cart is absolutely necessary for him. Robin of Bagshot, alias Gorgon, alias Bluff Bob, alias Carbuncle, alias Bob Booty.

SCENE IV

PEACHUM, MRS. PEACHUM.

Mrs. Peach.   What of Bob Booty, Husband? I hope nothing bad hath betided him. You know, my Dear, he's a favourite

Customer of mine. 'Twas he made me a Present of this Ring.

Peach. I have set his Name down in the Black-List, that's all, my Dear; he spends his Life among Women, and as soon as his Money is gone, one or other of the Ladies will hang him for the Reward, and there's forty Pound lost to us for ever.

Mrs. Peach. You know, my Dear, I never meddle in matters of Death; I always leave those Affairs to you. Women indeed are bitter bad Judges in these cases, for they are so partial to the Brave that they think every Man handsome who is going to the Camp or the Gallows.

AIR III. COLD AND RAW, &c.

If any Wench Venus's Girdle wear,
  Though she be never so ugly;
Lillys and Roses will quickly appear,
  And her Face look wond'rous smuggly.

Act I Scene IV

Beneath the left Ear so fit but a Cord,
(A Rope so charming a Zone is!)
The Youth in his Cart hath the Air of a Lord,
And we cry, There dies an Adonis!

But really, Husband, you should not be too hard-hearted, for you never had a finer, braver set of Men than at present. We have not had a Murder among them all, these seven Months. And truly, my Dear, that is a great Blessing.

Peach.   What a dickens is the Woman always a whimpering about Murder for? No Gentleman is ever look'd upon the worse for killing a Man in his own Defence; and if Business cannot be carried on without it, what would you have a Gentleman do?

Mrs. Peach.   If I am in the wrong, my Dear, you must excuse me, for No-body can help the Frailty of an over-scrupulous Conscience.

Peach.   Murder is as fashionable a Crime as a Man can be guilty of. How many fine Gentlemen have we in Newgate every Year, purely upon that Article! If they have wherewithal to persuade the Jury to bring it in Manslaughter, what are they the worse for it? So, my Dear, have done upon this Subject. Was Captain Macheath here this Morning, for the Bank-notes he left with you last Week?

Mrs. Peach.   Yes, my Dear; and though the Bank hath stopt Payment, he was so cheerful and so agreeable! Sure there is not a finer Gentleman upon the Road than the Captain! If he comes from Bagshot at any reasonable Hour he hath promis'd to make one this Evening with Polly and me, and Bob Booty, at a Party of Quadrille. Pray, my Dear, is the Captain rich?

Peach. The Captain keeps too good Company ever to grow rich. Marybone and the Chocolate-houses are his undoing. The Man that proposes to get Money by Play should have the Education of a fine Gentleman, and be train'd up to it from his Youth.

Mrs. Peach. Really, I am sorry upon Polly's Account the Captain hath not more Discretion. What business hath he to keep Company with Lords and Gentlemen? he should leave them to prey upon one another.

Peach. Upon Polly's Account! What, a Plague, does the Woman mean?—Upon Polly's Account!

Mrs. Peach. Captain Macheath is very fond of the Girl.

Peach. And what then?

Mrs. Peach. If I have any Skill in the Ways of Women, I am sure Polly thinks him a very pretty Man.

Peach. And what then? You would not be so mad to have the Wench marry him! Gamesters and Highwaymen are generally very good to their Whores, but they are very Devils to their Wives.

Mrs. Peach. But if Polly should be in love, how should we help her, or how can she help herself? Poor Girl, I am in the utmost Concern about her.

AIR IV. WHY IS YOUR FAITHFUL SLAVE DISDAIN'D? &c.

If Love the Virgin's Heart invade,
How, like a Moth, the simple Maid
Still plays about the Flame!

If soon she be not made a Wife,
Her Honour's sing'd, and then for Life,
She's—what I dare not name.

Peach. Look ye, Wife. A handsome Wench in our way of Business is as profitable as at the Bar of a Temple Coffee-House, who looks upon it as her livelihood to grant every Liberty but one. You see I would indulge the Girl as far as prudently we can. In any thing but Marriage! After that, my Dear, how shall we be safe? Are we not then in her Husband's Power? For a Husband hath the absolute Power over all a Wife's Secrets but her own. If the Girl had the Discretion of a Court Lady, who can have a dozen young Fellows at her Ear without complying with one, I should not matter it; but Polly is Tinder, and a Spark will at once set her on a Flame. Married! If the Wench does not know her own Profit, sure she knows her own Pleasure better than to make herself a Property! My Daughter to me should be, like a Court Lady to a Minister of State, a Key to the whole Gang. Married! If the Affair is not already done, I'll terrify her from it, by the example of our Neighbours.

Mrs. Peach.   May-hap, my Dear, you may injure the Girl. She loves to imitate the fine Ladies, and she may only allow the Captain Liberties in the View of Interest.

Peach.   But 'tis your Duty, my Dear, to warn the Girl against her Ruin, and to instruct her how to make the most of her Beauty. I'll go to her this moment, and sift her. In the mean time, Wife, rip out the Coronets and Marks of these dozen of Cambric Handkerchiefs, for I can dispose of them this Afternoon to a Chap in the City.

SCENE V

MRS. PEACHUM.

Never was a Man more out of the way in an Argument than my Husband! Why must our Polly, forsooth, differ from her Sex, and love only her Husband? And why must Polly's Marriage, contrary to all Observation, make her the less followed by other Men? All Men are Thieves in Love, and like a Woman the better for being another's Property.

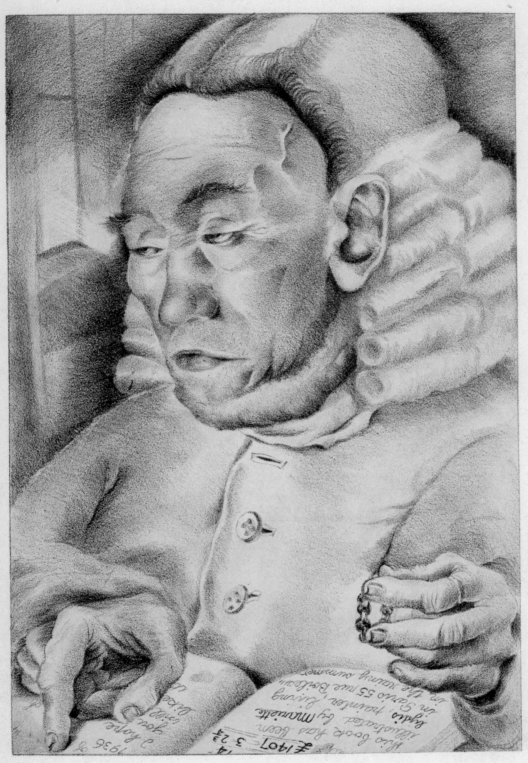

Peachum

AIR V. OF ALL THE SIMPLE THINGS WE DO, &c.

A Maid is like the golden oar,
Which hath Guineas intrinsical in't,
Whose Worth is never known, before
It is try'd and imprest in the Mint.

A Wife's like a Guinea in Gold,
Stampt with the Name of her Spouse;
Now here, now there; is bought, or is sold;
And is current in every House.

SCENE VI

MRS. PEACHUM, FILCH.

Mrs. Peach.   Come hither, Filch. I am as fond of this Child, as though my Mind misgave me he were my own. He hath as fine a Hand at picking a Pocket as a Woman, and is as nimble-finger'd as a Juggler. If an unlucky Session does not cut the

Rope of thy Life, I pronounce, Boy, thou wilt be a great Man in History. Where was your Post last Night, my Boy?

Filch. I ply'd at the Opera, Madam; and considering 'twas neither dark nor rainy, so that there was no great Hurry in getting Chairs and Coaches, made a tolerable hand on't. These seven Handkerchiefs, Madam.

Mrs. Peach. Colour'd ones, I see. They are of sure Sale from our Warehouse at Redress among the Seamen.

Filch. And this Snuff-box.

Mrs. Peach. Set in Gold! A pretty Encouragement this to a young Beginner.

Filch. I had a fair tug at a charming Gold Watch. Pox take the Taylors for making the Fobs so deep and narrow! It stuck by the way, and I was forc'd to make my Escape under a Coach. Really, Madam, I fear I shall be cut off in the Flower of my Youth, so that every now and then (since I was pumpt) I have thoughts of taking up and going to Sea.

Mrs. Peach. You should go to Hockley-in-the-Hole, and to Marybone, Child, to learn Valour. These are the Schools that have bred so many brave Men. I thought, Boy, by this time, thou hadst lost Fear as well as Shame. Poor Lad! how little does he know as yet of the Old Bailey! For the first Fact I'll insure thee from being hang'd; and going to Sea, Filch, will come time enough upon a Sentence of Transportation. But now, since you have nothing better to do, ev'n go to your Book, and learn your Catechism; for really a Man makes but an ill Figure in the Ordinary's Paper, who cannot give a satisfactory Answer to his Questions. But, hark you, my Lad. Don't tell me a Lye; for you know I hate a Lyar. Do you know of any thing that hath past between Captain Macheath and our Polly?

Filch. I beg you, Madam, don't ask me; for I must either tell a Lye to you or to Miss Polly; for I promis'd her I would not tell.

Mrs. Peach. But when the Honour of our Family is concern'd—

Filch. I shall lead a sad Life with Miss Polly, if ever she come to know that I told you. Besides, I would not willingly forfeit my own Honour by betraying any body.

Mrs. Peach. Yonder comes my Husband and Polly. Come, Filch, you shall go with me into my own Room, and tell me the whole Story. I'll give thee a most delicious Glass of a Cordial that I keep for my own drinking.

SCENE VII

PEACHUM, POLLY.

Polly. I know as well as any of the fine Ladies how to make the most of my self and of my Man too. A Woman knows how to be mercenary, though she hath never been in a Court or at an Assembly. We have it in our Natures, Papa. If I allow Captain Macheath some trifling Liberties, I have this Watch and other visible Marks of his Favour to show for it. A Girl who cannot grant some Things, and refuse what is most material, will make but a poor hand of her Beauty, and soon be thrown upon the Common.

AIR VI.   WHAT SHALL I DO TO SHOW HOW MUCH I LOVE HER, &c.

Virgins are like the fair Flower in its Lustre,
Which in the Garden enamels the Ground;
Near it the Bees in Play flutter and cluster,
And gaudy Butterflies frolick around.

But, when once pluck'd, 'tis no longer alluring,
To Covent-Garden 'tis sent, (as yet sweet),
There fades, and shrinks, and grows past all enduring,
Rots, stinks, and dies, and is trod under feet.

Peach.   You know, Polly, I am not against your toying and trifling with a Customer in the way of Business, or to get out a Secret, or so. But if I find out that you have play'd the fool and are married, you Jade you, I'll cut your Throat, Hussy. Now you know my Mind.

SCENE VIII

PEACHUM, POLLY, MRS. PEACHUM.

AIR VII.   OH, LONDON IS A FINE TOWN

MRS. PEACHUM, *in a very great Passion.*

Our Polly is a sad Slut! nor heeds what we taught her.
I wonder any Man alive will ever rear a Daughter!
For she must have both Hoods and Gowns, and Hoops to swell her
    Pride.
With Scarfs and Stays, and Gloves and Lace; and she will have Men
    beside;
And when she's drest with Care and Cost, all-tempting, fine and gay,
As Men should serve a Cowcumber, she flings herself away.
  Our Polly is a sad Slut, &c.

You Baggage! you Hussy! you inconsiderate Jade! had you been hang'd, it would not have vex'd me, for that might have been your Misfortune; but to do such a mad thing by Choice! The Wench is married, Husband.

Peach. Married! The Captain is a bold man, and will risque any thing for Money; to be sure he believes her a Fortune. Do you think your Mother and I should have liv'd comfortably so long together, if ever we had been married? Baggage!

Mrs. Peach. I knew she was always a proud Slut; and now the Wench hath play'd the Fool and married, because forsooth she should do like the Gentry. Can you support the expence of a Husband, Hussy, in gaming, drinking, and whoring? have you Money enough to carry on the daily Quarrels of Man and Wife about who shall squander most? There are not many Husbands and Wives, who can bear the Charges of plaguing one another in a handsome way. If you must be married, could you introduce no-body into our Family but a Highwayman? Why, thou foolish Jade, thou wilt be as ill-us'd, and as much neglected, as if thou hadst married a Lord!

Peach. Let not your Anger, my Dear, break through the Rules of Decency, for the Captain looks upon himself in the Military Capacity, as a Gentleman by his Profession. Besides what he hath already, I know he is in a fair way of getting, or of dying; and both these ways, let me tell you, are most excellent Chances for a Wife. Now pray tell me, Hussy, are you ruin'd or no?

Mrs. Peach. With Polly's Fortune, she might very well have gone off to a Person of Distinction. Yes, that you might, you pouting Slut!

Peach. What, is the Wench dumb? Speak, or I'll make you plead by squeezing out an Answer from you. Are you really bound Wife to him, or are you only upon liking? [*Pinches her.*

Polly. Oh!   [*Screaming.*

Mrs. Peach. How the Mother is to be pitied who hath handsome Daughters! Locks, Bolts, Bars, and Lectures of Morality are nothing to them: they break through them all. They have as much Pleasure in cheating a Father and Mother, as in cheating at Cards.

Peach. Why, Polly, I shall soon know if you are married, by Macheath's keeping from our House.

AIR VIII. GRIM KING OF THE GHOSTS, &c.

POLLY.   *Can Love be controul'd by Advice?*
Will Cupid our Mothers obey?
Though my Heart were as frozen as Ice,
    At his Flame 'twould have melted away.

When he kist me so closely he prest,
'Twas so sweet that I must have comply'd:
So I thought it both safest and best
To marry, for fear you should chide.

Mrs. Peach.   Then all the Hopes of our Family are gone for ever and ever!

Peach.   And Macheath may hang his Father and Mother-in-Law, in hope to get into their Daughter's Fortune.

Polly.   I did not marry him (as 'tis the Fashion) cooly and deliberately for Honour or Money. But, I love him.

Mrs. Peach.   Love him! Worse and worse! I thought the Girl had been better bred. Oh Husband, Husband! Her Folly makes me mad! My Head swims! I'm distracted! I can't support myself—Oh!   [*Faints.*

Peach.   See, Wench, to what a Condition you have reduc'd your poor Mother! a Glass of Cordial, this instant. How the poor Woman takes it to Heart!

                [POLLY *goes out, and returns with it.*
Ah, Hussy, now this is the only Comfort your Mother has left!

Polly.   Give her another Glass, Sir; my Mama drinks double the Quantity whenever she is out of Order. This, you see, fetches her.

Mrs. Peach.   The Girl shows such a Readiness, and so much Concern, that I could almost find in my Heart to forgive her.

Mrs.
Peachum

AIR IX. O JENNY, O JENNY, WHERE HAST THOU BEEN

O Polly, you might have toy'd and kist.
By keeping Men off, you keep them on.

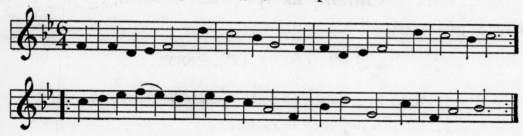

POLLY.   *But he so teaz'd me,*
And he so pleas'd me,
What I did, you must have done.

Mrs. Peach.   Not with a Highwayman.—You sorry Slut!

Peach.   A Word with you, Wife. 'Tis no new thing for a Wench to take Man without consent of Parents. You know 'tis the Frailty of Woman, my Dear.

Mrs. Peach.   Yes, indeed, the Sex is frail. But the first time a Woman is frail, she should be somewhat nice methinks, for then or never is the time to make her Fortune. After that, she hath nothing to do but to guard herself from being found out, and she may do what she pleases.

Peach.   Make your self a little easy; I have a Thought shall soon set all Matters again to rights. Why so melancholy, Polly? since what is done cannot be undone, we must all endeavour to make the best of it.

Mrs. Peach.   Well, Polly; as far as one Woman can forgive another, I forgive thee.—Your Father is too fond of you, Hussy.

Polly. Then all my Sorrows are at an end.

Mrs. Peach. A mighty likely Speech in troth, for a Wench who is just married!

AIR X. THOMAS, I CANNOT, &c.

POLLY. *I, like a Ship in Storms, was tost;*
Yet afraid to put in to Land;
For seiz'd in the Port the Vessel's lost,

Whose Treasure is contraband.
The Waves are laid,
My Duty's paid.
O Joy beyond Expression!
Thus, safe ashore,
I ask no more,
My All is in my Possession.

Peach.   I hear Customers in t'other Room; Go, talk with 'em, Polly; but come to us again, as soon as they are gone. But, heark ye, Child, if 'tis the Gentleman who was here Yesterday about the Repeating-Watch; say, you believe we can't get Intelligence of it, till to-morrow. For I lent it to Suky Straddle, to make a Figure with it to-night at a Tavern in Drury-Lane. If t'other Gentleman calls for the Silver-hilted Sword; you know Beetle-brow'd Jemmy hath it on, and he doth not come from Tunbridge till Tuesday Night; so that it cannot be had till then.

SCENE IX

PEACHUM, MRS. PEACHUM.

Peach.   Dear Wife, be a little pacified. Don't let your Passion run away with your Senses. Polly, I grant you, hath done a rash thing.

Mrs. Peach.   If she had had only an Intrigue with the Fellow, why the very best Families have excus'd and huddled up a Frailty of that sort. 'Tis Marriage, Husband, that makes it a blemish.

Peach.   But Money, Wife, is the true Fuller's Earth for Reputations, there is not a Spot or a Stain but what it can take out. A rich Rogue now-a-days is fit Company for any Gentleman; and the World, my Dear, hath not such a Contempt for Roguery as you imagine. I tell you, Wife, I can make this Match turn to our Advantage.

Mrs. Peach.   I am very sensible, Husband, that Captain Macheath is worth Money, but I am in doubt whether he hath not two or three Wives already, and then if he should dye in a Session or two, Polly's Dower would come into Dispute.

Peach.   That, indeed, is a Point which ought to be consider'd.

AIR XI.   A SOLDIER AND A SAILOR

A Fox may steal your Hens, Sir,
A Whore your Health and Pence, Sir,
Your Daughter rob your Chest, Sir,

Your Wife may steal your Rest, Sir,
  A Thief your Goods and Plate.
But this is all but picking;
With Rest, Pence, Chest, and Chicken,
It ever was decreed, Sir,
If Lawyer's Hand is fee'd, Sir,
  He steals your whole Estate.

The Lawyers are bitter Enemies to those in our Way. They don't care that any body should get a Clandestine Livelihood but themselves.

SCENE X

MRS. PEACHUM, PEACHUM, POLLY.

Polly.   'Twas only Nimming Ned. He brought in a Damask Window-Curtain, a Hoop-Petticoat, a Pair of Silver Candlesticks, a Perriwig, and one Silk Stocking, from the Fire that happen'd last Night.

Peach.   There is not a Fellow that is cleverer in his way, and saves more Goods out of the Fire than Ned. But now, Polly, to your Affair; for Matters must not be left as they are. You are married then, it seems?

Polly.   Yes, Sir.

Peach.   And how do you propose to live, Child?

Polly.   Like other Women, Sir, upon the Industry of my Husband.

Mrs. Peach.　What, is the Wench turn'd Fool? A Highway-man's Wife, like a Soldier's, hath as little of his Pay, as of his Company.

Peach.　And had not you the common Views of a Gentle-woman in your Marriage, Polly?

Polly.　I don't know what you mean, Sir.

Peach.　Of a Jointure, and of being a Widow.

Polly.　But I love him, Sir: how then could I have Thoughts of parting with him?

Peach.　Parting with him! Why, that is the whole Scheme and Intention of all Marriage Articles. The comfortable Estate of Widow-hood, is the only hope that keeps up a Wife's Spirits. Where is the Woman who would scruple to be a Wife, if she had it in her Power to be a widow whenever she pleas'd? If you have any Views of this sort, Polly, I shall think the Match not so very unreasonable.

Polly.　How I dread to hear your Advice! Yet I must beg you to explain yourself.

Peach.　Secure what he hath got, have him peach'd the next Sessions, and then at once you are made a rich Widow.

Polly.　What, murder the Man I love! The Blood runs cold at my Heart with the very Thought of it.

Peach.　Fye, Polly! What hath Murder to do in the Affair? Since the thing sooner or later must happen, I dare say, the Captain himself would like that we should get the Reward for his Death sooner than a Stranger. Why, Polly, the Captain knows that as 'tis his Employment to rob, so 'tis ours to take

Robbers; every man in his Business. So that there is no Malice in the Case.

Mrs. Peach.   Ay, Husband, now you have nick'd the Matter. To have him peach'd is the only thing could ever make me forgive her.

AIR XII.   NOW PONDER WELL, YE PARENTS DEAR

POLLY.   *Oh, ponder well! be not severe;*
So save a wretched Wife!
For on the Rope that hangs my Dear
Depends poor Polly's Life.

Mrs. Peach.   But your Duty to your Parents, Hussy, obliges you to hang him. What would many a Wife give for such an Opportunity!

Polly.   What is a Jointure, what is Widow-hood to me? I know my Heart. I cannot survive him.

AIR XIII.   *Le printemps rappelle aux armes*

The Turtle thus with plaintive crying,
Her Lover dying,

> *The Turtle thus with plaintive crying,*
> *Laments her Dove.*
> *Down she drops quite spent with sighing,*
> *Pair'd in Death, as pair'd in Love.*

Thus, Sir, it will happen to your poor Polly.

Mrs. Peach. What, is the Fool in love in earnest then? I hate thee for being particular: Why, Wench, thou art a Shame to thy very Sex.

Polly. But hear me, Mother. If you ever lov'd—

Mrs. Peach. Those cursed Playbooks she reads have been her Ruin. One Word more, Hussy, and I shall knock your Brains out, if you have any.

Peach. Keep out of the way, Polly, for fear of Mischief, and consider of what is propos'd to you.

Mrs. Peach. Away, Hussy. Hang your Husband, and be dutiful.

Polly
Peachum

SCENE XI

MRS. PEACHUM, PEACHUM.

[POLLY *listening.*

Mrs. Peach. The Thing, Husband, must and shall be done. For the sake of Intelligence we must take other Measures, and have him peach'd the next Session without her Consent. If she will not know her Duty, we know ours.

Peach. But really, my Dear, it grieves one's Heart to take off a great Man. When I consider his Personal Bravery, his fine Stratagem, how much we have already got by him, and how much more we may get, methinks I can't find in my Heart to have a Hand in his Death. I wish you could have made Polly undertake it.

Mrs. Peach. But in a Case of Necessity—our own Lives are in danger.

Peach. Then, indeed, we must comply with the Customs of the World, and make Gratitude give way to Interest.—He shall be taken off.

Mrs. Peach. I'll undertake to manage Polly.

Peach. And I'll prepare Matters for the Old Bailey.

SCENE XII

Polly. Now I'm a Wretch, indeed.—Methinks I see him already in the Cart, sweeter and more lovely than the Nosegay in his Hand!—I hear the Crowd extolling his Resolution and

Intrepidity!—What Vollies of Sighs are sent from the Windows of Holborn, that so comely a Youth should be brought to disgrace!—I see him at the Tree! The whole Circle are in Tears!—even Butchers weep!—Jack Ketch himself hesitates to perform his Duty, and would be glad to lose his Fee, by a Reprieve. What then will become of Polly!—As yet I may inform him of their Design, and aid him in his Escape.—It shall be so. —But then he flies, absents himself, and I bar myself from his dear, dear Conversation! That too will distract me.—If he keep out of the way, my Papa and Mama may in time relent, and we may be happy.—If he stays, he is hang'd, and then he is lost for ever!—He intended to lye conceal'd in my Room, 'till the Dusk of the Evening: if they are abroad, I'll this Instant let him out, lest some Accident should prevent him.

[Exit, and returns.

SCENE XIII

POLLY, MACHEATH.

AIR XIV. PRETTY PARROT, SAY—

MACH.　*Pretty Polly, say,*
When I was away,
Did your Fancy never stray
To some newer Lover?
POLLY.　*Without Disguise,*
Heaving Sighs,

Doating Eyes,
My constant Heart discover.
Fondly let me loll!
MACH.   *O pretty, pretty Poll.*

Polly.   And are *you* as fond as ever, my Dear?

Mach.   Suspect my Honour, my Courage, suspect any thing but my Love. May my Pistols miss Fire, and my Mare slip her Shoulder while I am pursu'd, if I ever forsake thee!

Polly.   Nay, my Dear, I have no Reason to doubt you, for I find in the Romance you lent me, none of the great Heroes were ever false in Love.

The Beggar's Opera

AIR XV. PRAY, FAIR ONE, BE KIND—

MACH. *My heart was so free,*
It rov'd like the Bee,
'Till Polly my Passion requited;
I sipt each Flower,
I chang'd ev'ry Hour,
But here ev'ry Flower is United.

Polly. Were you sentenc'd to Transportation, sure, my Dear, you could not leave me behind you—could you?

Mach. Is there any Power, any Force that could tear me from thee? You might sooner tear a Pension out of the Hands of a Courtier, a Fee from a Lawyer, a pretty Woman from a Looking-glass, or any Woman from Quadrille. But to tear me from thee is impossible!

AIR XVI. OVER THE HILLS AND FAR AWAY

Were I laid on Greenland's Coast
And in my Arms embrac'd my Lass;

Warm amidst eternal Frost,

Too soon the Half Year's Night would pass.

POLLY. *Were I sold on Indian Soil,*

Soon as the burning Day was clos'd,

I could mock the sultry Toil,

When on my Charmer's Breast repos'd.

MACH. *And I would love you all the Day,*

POLLY. *Every Night would kiss and play,*

MACH. *If with me you'd fondly stray*

POLLY. *Over the Hills and far away.*

Polly. Yes, I would go with thee. But oh!—how shall I speak it? I must be torn from thee. We must part.

Mach. How! Part!

Polly. We must, we must. My Papa and Mama are set against thy Life. They now, even now, are in Search after thee.

They are preparing Evidence against Thee. Thy Life depends upon a Moment.

AIR XVII. GIN THOU WERT MINE AWN THING—

O what Pain it is to part!
Can I leave thee, can I leave thee?
O what Pain it is to part!

Can thy Polly ever leave thee?
But lest Death my Love should thwart,
And bring thee to the fatal Cart,
Thus I tear thee from my bleeding Heart!
Fly hence, and let me leave thee.

One Kiss and then—one Kiss—begone—farewell.

Mach.   My Hand, my Heart, my Dear, is so riveted to thine, that I cannot unloose my Hold.

Polly. But my Papa may intercept thee, and then I should lose the very glimmering of Hope. A few Weeks, perhaps, may reconcile us all. Shall thy Polly hear from thee?

Mach. Must I then go?

Polly. And will not Absence change your Love?

Mach. If you doubt it, let me stay—and be hang'd.

Polly. Oh, how I fear! How I tremble!—Go—but when Safety will give you leave, you will be sure to see me again; for 'till then Polly is wretched.

[*Parting, and looking back at each other with fondness; he at one Door, she at the other.*

AIR XVIII. O THE BROOM, &c.

MACH. *The Miser thus a Shilling sees,*
Which he's oblig'd to pay,
With Sighs resigns it by degrees,
And fears 'tis gone for aye.

POLLY. *The Boy, thus, when his Sparrow's flown,*
The Bird in Silence eyes;
But soon as out of Sight 'tis gone,
Whines, whimpers, sobs and cries.

ACT II SCENE I

A Tavern near Newgate

JEMMY TWITCHER, CROOK-FINGER'D JACK, WAT DREARY, ROBIN OF BAGSHOT, NIMMING NED, HENRY PADINGTON, MATT OF THE MINT, BEN BUDGE, *and the rest of the* GANG, *at the Table, with Wine, Brandy and Tobacco.*

Ben. But pr'ythee, Matt, what is become of thy Brother Tom? I have not seen him since my Return from Transportation.

Matt. Poor Brother Tom had an Accident this time Twelvemonth, and so clever a made Fellow he was, that I could not save him from those fleaing Rascals the Surgeons; and now, poor Man, he is among the Otamys at Surgeon's Hall.

Ben. So it seems his Time was come.

Jem. But the present Time is ours, and no Body alive hath more. Why are the Laws levell'd at us? Are we more dishonest than the rest of Mankind? What we win, Gentlemen, is our own by the Law of Arms, and the Right of Conquest.

Crook. Where shall we find such another Set of practical Philosophers, who to a Man are above the Fear of Death?

Wat. Sound Men, and true!

Robin. Of try'd Courage, and indefatigable Industry!

Ned. Who is there here that would not dye for his Friend?

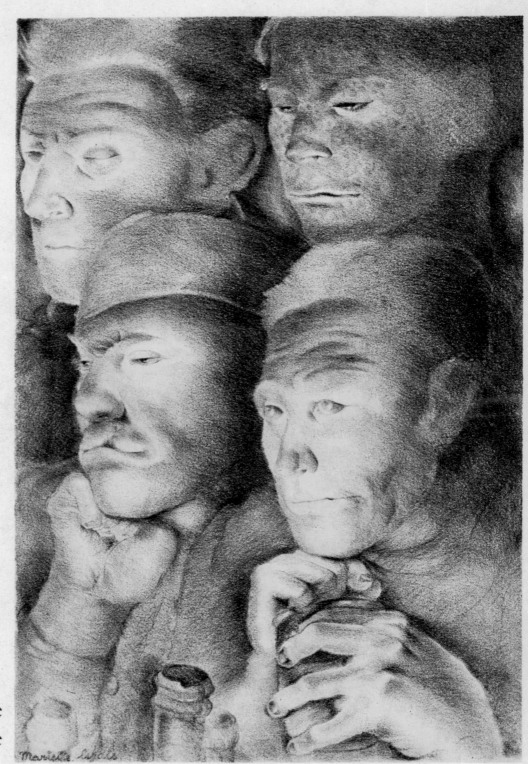

The
Conference

Harry. Who is there here that would betray him for his Interest?

Matt. Show me a Gang of Courtiers that can say as much.

Ben. We are for a just Partition of the World, for every Man hath a Right to enjoy Life.

Matt. We retrench the Superfluities of Mankind. The World is avaricious, and I hate Avarice. A covetous fellow, like a Jackdaw, steals what he was never made to enjoy, for the sake of hiding it. These are the Robbers of Mankind, for Money was made for the Free-hearted and Generous, and where is the injury of taking from another, what he hath not the Heart to make use of?

Jem. Our several Stations for the Day are fixt. Good luck attend us all. Fill the Glasses.

AIR I. FILL EV'RY GLASS, &c.

MATT. *Fill ev'ry Glass, for Wine inspires us,*
And fires us

With Courage, Love and Joy.
Women and Wine should Life employ.
Is there ought else on Earth desirous?
CHORUS.   *Fill ev'ry Glass, &c.*

SCENE II

To them enter MACHEATH.

Mach.   Gentlemen, well met. My Heart hath been with you this Hour; but an unexpected Affair hath detain'd me. No Ceremony, I beg you.

Matt.   We were just breaking up to go upon Duty. Am I to have the Honour of taking the Air with you, Sir, this Evening upon the Heath? I drink a Dram now and then with the Stage-Coachmen in the way of Friendship and Intelligence; and I know that about this Time there will be Passengers upon the Western Road, who are worth speaking with.

Mach.   I was to have been of that Party—but—

Matt.   But what, Sir?

Mach.   Is there any man who suspects my Courage?

Matt.   We have all been witnesses of it.

Mach.   My Honour and Truth to the Gang?

Matt.   I'll be answerable for it.

Mach.   In the Division of our Booty, have I ever shown the least Marks of Avarice or Injustice?

Matt.   By these Questions something seems to have ruffled you. Are any of us suspected?

Mach.　I have a fixt Confidence, Gentlemen, in you all, as Men of Honour, and as such I value and respect you. Peachum is a Man that is useful to us.

Matt.　Is he about to play us any foul Play? I'll shoot him through the Head.

Mach.　I beg you, Gentlemen, act with Conduct and Discretion. A Pistol is your last resort.

Matt.　He knows nothing of this Meeting.

Mach.　Business cannot go on without him. He is a Man who knows the World, and is a necessary Agent to us. We have had a slight Difference, and till it is accommodated I shall be oblig'd to keep out of his way. Any private Dispute of mine shall be of no ill consequence to my Friends. You must continue to act under his Direction, for the moment we break loose from him, our Gang is ruin'd.

Matt.　As a Bawd to a Whore, I grant you, he is to us of great Convenience.

Mach.　Make him believe I have quitted the Gang, which I can never do but with Life. At our private Quarters I will continue to meet you. A Week or so will probably reconcile us.

Matt.　Your Instructions shall be observ'd. 'Tis now high time for us to repair to our several Duties; so till the Evening at our Quarters in Moor-fields we bid you farewell.

Mach.　I shall wish my self with you. Success attend you.

[*Sits down melancholy at the Table.*

AIR II. MARCH IN RINALDO, WITH DRUMS AND TRUMPETS

MATT.   *Let us take the Road.*
Hark! I hear the sound of Coaches!
The hour of Attack approaches,
To your Arms, brave Boys, and load.

See the Ball I hold!
Let the Chymists toil like Asses,
Our fire their fire surpasses,
And turns all our Lead to Gold.

[The GANG, *rang'd in the Front of the Stage, load their Pistols, and stick them under their Girdles; then go off singing the first Part in Chorus.*

SCENE III

MACHEATH, DRAWER.

Mach.   What a Fool is a fond Wench! Polly is most confoundedly bit.—I love the Sex. And a Man who loves Money, might as well be contented with one Guinea, as I with one Woman. The Town perhaps hath been as much oblig'd to me, for recruiting it with free-hearted Ladies, as to any Recruiting Officer in the Army. If it were not for us and the other Gentlemen of the Sword, Drury-Lane would be uninhabited.

AIR III.   WOULD YOU HAVE A YOUNG VIRGIN, &c.

If the Heart of a Man is deprest with Cares,
The Mist is dispell'd when a Woman appears;
Like the Notes of a Fiddle, she sweetly, sweetly
Raises the Spirits, and charms our Ears.

Roses and Lillies her Cheeks disclose,
But her ripe Lips are more sweet than those.
    Press her,
    Caress her
    With Blisses,
    Her Kisses
Dissolve us in Pleasure, and soft Repose.

I must have Women. There is nothing unbends the Mind like them. Money is not so strong a Cordial for the Time, Drawer.

Enter DRAWER.

Is the Potter gone for all the Ladies, according to directions?
    Draw.   I expect him back every Minute. But you know, Sir, you sent him as far as Hockey-in-the-Hole, for three of the Ladies, for one in Vinegar Yard, and for the rest of them somewhere about Lewkner's Lane. Sure some of them are below, for I hear the Barr Bell. As they come I will show them up. Coming, coming.

SCENE IV

MACHEATH, MRS. COAXER, DOLLY TRULL, MRS. VIXEN, BETTY DOXY, JENNY DIVER, MRS. SLAMMEKIN, SUKY TAWDRY, *and* MOLLY BRAZEN.

Mach.   Dear Mrs. Coaxer, you are welcome. You look charmingly to-day. I hope you don't want the Repairs of Quality, and lay on Paint.—Dolly Trull! kiss me, you Slut; are you as amorous as ever, Hussy? You are always so taken up with stealing Hearts, that you don't allow your self Time to steal any thing else.—Ah Dolly, thou wilt ever be a Coquette!—Mrs. Vixen, I'm yours, I always lov'd a Woman of Wit and Spirit; they make charming Mistresses, but plaguy Wives.—Betty Doxy! Come hither, Hussy. Do you drink as hard as ever? You had better stick to good Wholesome Beer; for in troth, Betty, Strong-Waters will in time ruin your Constitution. You should leave those to your Betters.—What! and my pretty Jenny Diver too! As prim and demure as ever! There is not any Prude, though ever so high bred, hath a more sanctify'd Look, with a more mischievous Heart. Ah! thou art a dear artful Hypocrite. —Mrs. Slammekin! as careless and genteel as ever! all you fine Ladies, who know your own Beauty, affect an Undress.—But see, here's Suky Tawdry come to contradict what I was saying. Every thing she gets one way she lays out upon her Back. Why Suky, you must keep at least a dozen Tallymen. Molly Brazen! [*She kisses him.*] That's well done. I love a free-hearted Wench. Thou hast a most agreeable Assurance, Girl, and art as willing as a Turtle.— But hark! I hear musick. The Harper is at the Door. If Musick be the Food of Love, play on. E'er you seat your selves, Ladies, what think you of a Dance? Come in.

Enter HARPER.

Play the French Tune, that Mrs. Slammekin was so fond of.
  [*A Dance à la ronde in the French Manner; near the End of it this Song and Chorus.*

AIR IV. COTILLON

Youth's the Season made for Joys,
Love is then our Duty,
She alone who that employs,
Well deserves her Beauty.
Let's be gay,
While we may,
Beauty's a Flower, despis'd in decay.
Youth's the Season, &c.

Let us drink and sport to-day,
Ours is not to-morrow.
Love with Youth flies swift away,
Age is nought but Sorrow.
Dance and sing,
Time's on the Wing,
Life never knows the return of Spring.

CHORUS.   *Let us drink, &c.*

A dance
"à la ronde"
in the
French
manner

Mach.   Now pray, Ladies, take your Places. Here Fellow, [*Pays the* HARPER.] Bid the Drawer bring us more Wine.

[*Exit* HARPER.

If any of the Ladies chuse Ginn, I hope they will be so free to call for it.

Jenny.   You look as if you meant me. Wine is strong enough for me. Indeed, Sir, I never drink Strong-Waters, but when I have the Cholic.

Mach.   Just the Excuse of the fine Ladies! Why, a Lady of Quality is never without the Cholic. I hope, Mrs. Coaxer, you have had good Success of late in your Visits among the Mercers.

Coax.   We have so many Interlopers—yet with Industry, one may still have a little Picking. I carried a silver flower'd Lutestring and a Piece of black Padesoy to Mr. Peachum's Lock but last Week.

Vix.   There's Molly Brazen hath the Ogle of a Rattle-Snake. She rivetted a Linnen-draper's Eye so fast upon her, that he was nick'd of three Pieces of Cambric before he could look off.

Braz.   Oh dear Madam!—But sure nothing can come up to your handling of Laces! And then you have such a sweet deluding Tongue! To cheat a Man is nothing; but the Woman must have fine Parts indeed who cheats a Woman!

Vix.   Lace, Madam, lyes in a small Compass, and is of easy Conveyance. But you are apt, Madam, to think too well of your Friends.

Coax.   If any Woman hath more Art than another, to be sure, 'tis Jenny Diver. Though her Fellow be never so agreeable, she can pick his Pocket as cooly, as if Money were her only Pleasure. Now that is a Command of the Passions uncommon in a Woman!

Jenny.   I never go to the Tavern with a Man, but in the View of Business. I have other Hours, and other sort of Men for my Pleasure. But had I your Address, Madam—

Mach.   Have done with your Compliments, Ladies; and drink about: you are not so fond of me, Jenny, as you use to be.

Jenny.   'Tis not convenient, Sir, to show my Fondness among so many Rivals. 'Tis your own Choice, and not the warmth of my Inclination, that will determine you.

AIR V. ALL IN A MISTY MORNING, &c.

Before the Barn-door crowing,
The Cock by Hens attended,

His Eyes around him throwing,
Stands for a while suspended.
Then One he singles from the Crew,
And cheers the happy Hen;
With how do you do, and how do you do,
And how do you do again.

Mach.   Ah Jenny! thou art a dear Slut.

Trull.   Pray, Madam, were you ever in keeping?

Tawd.   I hope, Madam, I han't been so long upon the Town, but I have met with some good Fortune as well as my Neighbours.

Trull.   Pardon me, Madam, I meant no harm by the Question; 'twas only in the way of Conversation.

Tawd.   Indeed, Madam, if I had not been a Fool, I might have liv'd very handsomely with my last Friend. But upon his missing five Guineas, he turn'd me off. Now I never suspected he had counted them.

Slam.   Who do you look upon as your best sort of Keepers?

Trull.   That, Madam, is thereafter as they be.

Slam.   I, Madam, was once kept by a Jew; and bating their Religion, to Women they are a good sort of People.

Tawd.   Now for my part, I own I like an old Fellow: for we always make them pay for what they can't do.

Vix.   A spruce Prentice, let me tell you, Ladies, is no ill thing, they bleed freely. I have sent at least two or three dozen of them in my time to the Plantations.

Jen. But to be sure, Sir, with so much good Fortune as you have had upon the Road, you must be grown immensely rich.

Mach. The Road, indeed, hath done me justice, but the Gaming-Table hath been my ruin.

AIR VI. WHEN ONCE I LAY WITH ANOTHER
MAN'S WIFE, &c.

JEN.   *The Gamesters and Lawyers are Jugglers alike,*
If they meddle your All is in danger.
Like Gypsies, if once they can finger a Souse,
Your Pockets they pick, and they pilfer your House,
And give your Estate to a Stranger.

These are the Tools of a Man of Honour. Cards and Dice are only fit for cowardly Cheats, who prey upon their Friends.
            [*She takes up his Pistol.* TAWDRY *takes up the other.*
Tawd. This, Sir, is fitter for your Hand. Besides your loss of Money, 'tis a Loss to the Ladies. Gaming takes you off from Women. How fond could I be of you! but before Company, 'tis ill bred.

Mach. Wanton Hussies!

Jen.   I must and will have a Kiss to give my Wine a zest.

[*They take him about the Neck, and make Signs to* PEACHUM *and* CONSTABLES, *who rush in upon him.*

SCENE V

To them, PEACHUM *and* CONSTABLES.

Peach.   I seize you, Sir, as my Prisoner.

Mach.   Was this well done, Jenny?—Women are Decoy Ducks; who can trust them! Beasts, Jades, Jilts, Harpies, Furies, Whores!

Peach.   Your Case, Mr. Macheath, is not particular. The greatest Heroes have been ruin'd by Women. But, to do them justice, I must own they are a pretty sort of Creatures, if we could trust them. You must now, Sir, take your leave of the Ladies, and if they have a Mind to make you a Visit, they will be sure to find you at home. The Gentleman, Ladies, lodges in Newgate. Constables, wait upon the Captain to his Lodgings.

AIR VII.   WHEN FIRST I LAID SIEGE TO MY CHLORIS, &c.

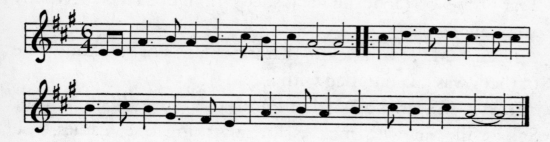

MAC.   *At the Tree I shall suffer with pleasure,*
At the Tree I shall suffer with pleasure,
Let me go where I will,
In all kinds of Ill,
I shall find no such Furies as these are.

Peach.   Ladies, I'll take care the Reckoning shall be discharg'd.

[*Exit* MACHEATH, *guarded with* PEACHUM *and* CONSTABLES.

SCENE VI

The WOMEN *remain.*

Vix.   Look ye, Mrs. Jenny, though Mr. Peachum may have made a private Bargain with you and Suky Tawdry for betraying the Captain, as we were all assisting, we ought all to share alike.

Coax.   I think Mr. Peachum, after so long an acquaintance, might have trusted me as well as Jenny Diver.

Slam.   I am sure at least three Men of his hanging, and in a Year's time too (if he did me justice) should be set down to my account.

Trull.   Mrs. Slammekin, that is not fair. For you know one of them was taken in Bed with me.

Jenny.   As far as a Bowl of Punch or a Treat, I believe Mrs. Suky will join with me. As for any thing else, Ladies, you cannot in conscience expect it.

Slam.   Dear Madam—

Trull.   I would not for the World—

Slam.   'Tis impossible for me—

Trull.   As I hope to be sav'd, Madam—

Slam.   Nay, then I must stay here all Night—

Trull.   Since you command me.

[*Exeunt with great Ceremony.*

SCENE VII

Newgate

LOCKIT, TURNKEYS, MACHEATH, CONSTABLES.

Lock.   Noble Captain, you are welcome. You have not been a Lodger of mine this Year and a-half. You know the custom, Sir. Garnish, Captain, Garnish. Hand me down those Fetters there.

Mach.   Those, Mr. Lockit, seem to be the heaviest of the whole sett. With your leave, I should like the further pair better.

Lock.   Look ye, Captain, we know what is fittest for our Prisoners. When a Gentleman uses me with Civility, I always do the best I can to please him.—Hand them down, I say.—We have them of all Prices, from one Guinea to ten, and 'tis fitting every Gentleman should please himself.

Mach.   I understand you, Sir. [*Gives Money.*] The Fees here are so many, and so exorbitant, that few Fortunes can bear the

Expence of getting off handsomely, or of dying like a Gentleman.

Lock.   Those, I see, will fit the Captain better.—Take down the further Pair. Do but examine them, Sir.—Never was better work.—How genteely they are made!—They will fit as easy as a Glove, and the nicest Man in England might not be asham'd to wear them. [*He puts on the Chains.*] If I had the best Gentleman in the Land in my Custody I could not equip him more handsomely. And so, Sir—I now leave you to your private Meditations.

SCENE VIII

MACHEATH.

AIR VIII.   COURTIERS, COURTIERS THINK IT NO HARM, &c.

Man may escape from Rope and Gun
Nay, some have out-liv'd the Doctor's Pill;

Who takes a Woman must be undone,
That Basilisk is sure to kill.

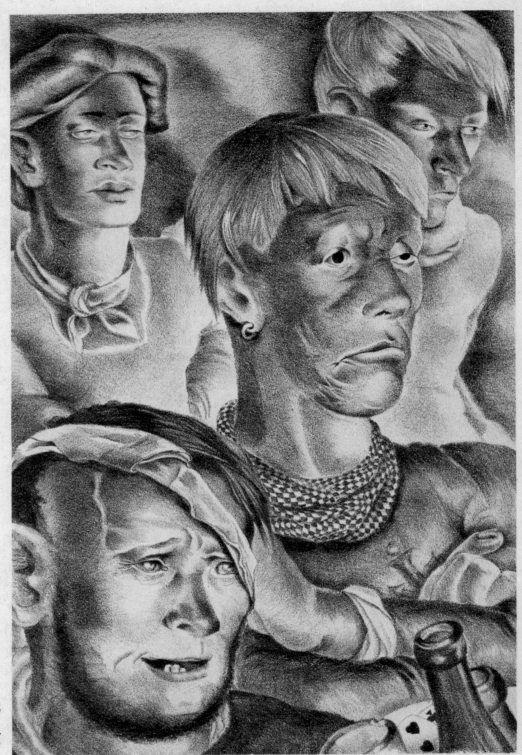

Macheath's
Gang

The Fly that sips Treacle is lost in the Sweets,
So he that tastes Woman, Woman, Woman,
He that tastes Woman, Ruin meets.

To what a woful plight have I brought my self! Here must I (all day long, 'till I am hang'd) be confin'd to hear the Reproaches of a Wench who lays her Ruin at my Door. I am in the Custody of her Father, and to be sure if he knows of the matter, I shall have a fine time on't betwixt this and my Execution. But I promis'd the Wench Marriage. What signifies a Promise to a Woman? Does not Man in Marriage itself promise a hundred things that he never means to perform? Do all we can, Women will believe us; for they look upon a Promise as an Excuse for following their own Inclinations.—But here comes Lucy, and I cannot get from her. Wou'd I were deaf!

SCENE IX

MACHEATH, LUCY.

Lucy. You base Man you,—how can you look me in the Face after what hath past between us? See here, perfidious Wretch, how I am forc'd to bear about the load of Infamy you have laid upon me. O Macheath! thou hast robb'd me of my Quiet—to see thee tortur'd would give me pleasure.

AIR IX. A LOVELY LASS TO A FRIAR CAME, &c.

Thus when a good Huswife sees a Rat
In her Trap in the Morning taken,

With pleasure her Heart goes pit a pat,
In Revenge for her loss of Bacon.
Then she throws him
To the Dog or Cat,
To be worried, crush'd and shaken.

Mac. Have you no Bowels, no Tenderness, my dear Lucy, to see a Husband in these Circumstances?

Lucy. A Husband!

Mac. In ev'ry respect but the Form, and that, my Dear, may be said over us at any time. Friends should not insist upon Ceremonies. From a Man of honour, his Word is as good as his Bond.

Lucy. 'Tis the pleasure of all you fine Men to insult the Women you have ruin'd.

AIR X. 'TWAS WHEN THE SEA WAS ROARING, &c.

How cruel are the Traytors,
Who lye and swear in jest,

To cheat unguarded Creatures
Of Virtue, Fame, and Rest!
Whoever steals a Shilling,

Through shame the Guilt conceals:
In Love the perjur'd Villain
With Boasts the Theft reveals.

Mac. The very first opportunity, my Dear, (have but patience) you shall be my Wife in whatever manner you please.

Lucy. Insinuating Monster! And so you think I know nothing of the Affair of Miss Polly Peachum.—I could tear thy Eyes out!

Mac. Sure Lucy, you can't be such a Fool as to be jealous of Polly!

Lucy. Are you not married to her, you Brute, you?

Mac.   Married! Very good. The Wench gives it out only to vex thee, and to ruin me in thy good Opinion. 'Tis true, I go to the House; I chat with the Girl, I kiss her, I say a thousand things to her (as all Gentlemen do) that mean nothing, to divert my self; and now the silly Jade hath set it about that I am married to her, to let me know what she would be at. Indeed, my dear Lucy, these violent Passions may be of ill consequence to a Woman in your condition.

Lucy.   Come, come, Captain, for all your Assurance, you know that Miss Polly hath put it out of your power to do me the Justice you promis'd me.

Mac.   A jealous Woman believes ev'ry thing her Passion suggests. To convince you of my Sincerity, if we can find the Ordinary, I shall have no scruples of making you my Wife; and I know the consequence of having two at a time.

Lucy.   That you are only to be hang'd, and so get rid of them both.

Mac.   I am ready, my dear Lucy, to give you satisfaction—if you think there is any in Marriage. What can Man of Honour say more?

Lucy.   So then it seems, you are not married to Miss Polly.

Mac.   You know, Lucy, the Girl is prodigiously conceited. No Man can say a civil thing to her, but (like other fine Ladies) her Vanity makes her think he's her own for ever and ever.

Act II Scene IX

AIR XI. THE SUN HAD LOOS'D HIS WEARY TEAMS, &c.

The first time at the Looking-glass
The Mother sets her Daughter,
The Image strikes the smiling Lass
With Self-love ever after.

Each time she looks, she, fonder grown,
Thinks ev'ry Charm grows stronger.
But alas, vain Maid, all Eyes but your own
Can see you are not younger.

When Women consider their own Beauties, they are all alike unreasonable in their demands; for they expect their Lovers should like them as long as they like themselves.

Lucy.   Yonder is my Father—perhaps this way we may light upon the Ordinary, who shall try if you will be as good as your Word.—For I long to be made an honest Woman.

SCENE X

PEACHUM, LOCKIT *with an Account-Book.*

Lock. In this last Affair, Brother Peachum, we are agreed. You have consented to go halves in Macheath.

Peach. We shall never fall out about an Execution.—But as to that Article, pray how stands our last Year's account?

Lock. If you will run your Eye over it, you'll find 'tis fair and clearly stated.

Peach. This long Arrear of the Government is very hard upon us! Can it be expected that we should hang our Acquaintance for nothing, when our Betters will hardly save theirs without being paid for it? Unless the People in employment pay better, I promise them for the future, I shall let other Rogues live besides their own.

Lock. Perhaps, Brother, they are afraid these matters may be carried too far. We are treated too by them with Contempt, as if our Profession were not reputable.

Peach. In one respect indeed, our Employment may be reckon'd dishonest, because, like Great Statesmen, we encourage those who betray their Friends.

Lock. Such Language, Brother, any where else, might turn to your prejudice. Learn to be more guarded, I beg you.

AIR XII. HOW HAPPY ARE WE, &c.

When you censure the Age,
Be cautious and sage,
Lest the Courtiers offended should be:
If you mention Vice or Bribe,
'Tis so pat to all the Tribe;
Each crys—That was levell'd at me.

Peach. Here's poor Ned Clincher's Name, I see. Sure, Brother Lockit, there was a little unfair proceeding in Ned's case: for he told me in the Condemn'd Hold, that for Value receiv'd, you had promis'd him a Session or two longer without Molestation.

Lock. Mr. Peachum—This is the first time my Honour was ever call'd in Question.

Peach. Business is at an end—if once we act dishonourably.

Lock. Who accuses me?

Peach. You are warm, Brother.

Lock. He that attacks my Honour, attacks my Livelihood.
—And this Usage—Sir—is not to be born.

Peach. Since you provoke me to speak—I must tell you too,

that Mrs. Coaxer charges you with defrauding her of her Information-Money, for the apprehending of curl-pated Hugh. Indeed, indeed, Brother, we must punctually pay our Spies, or we shall have no Information.

Lock. Is this Language to me, Sirrah—who have sav'd you from the Gallows, Sirrah! [*Collaring each other.*

Peach. If I am hang'd, it shall be for ridding the World of an arrant Rascal.

Lock. This Hand shall do the office of the Halter you deserve, and throttle you—you Dog!—

Peach. Brother, Brother—we are both in the Wrong—we shall be both Losers in the Dispute—for you know we have it in our Power to hang each other. You should not be so passionate.

Lock. Nor you so provoking.

Peach. 'Tis our mutual Interest; 'tis for the Interest of the World we should agree. If I said any thing, Brother, to the Prejudice of your Character, I ask pardon.

Lock. Brother Peachum—I can forgive as well as resent. Give me your Hand. Suspicion does not become a Friend.

Peach. I only meant to give you occasion to justifie yourself: But I must now step home, for I expect the Gentleman about this Snuff-box, that Filch nimm'd two Nights ago in the Park. I appointed him at this hour.

Captain
Macheath

SCENE XI

LOCKIT, LUCY.

Lock. Whence come you, Hussy?

Lucy. My Tears might answer that Question.

Lock. You have then been whimpering and fondling, like a Spaniel, over the Fellow that hath abus'd you.

Lucy. One can't help Love; one can't cure it. 'Tis not in my Power to obey you, and hate him.

Lock. Learn to bear your Husband's Death like a reasonable Woman. 'Tis not the fashion, now-a-days, so much as to affect Sorrow upon these Occasions. No Woman would ever marry, if she had not the Chance of Mortality for a Release. Act like a Woman of Spirit, Hussy, and thank your Father for what he is doing.

AIR XIII. OF A NOBLE RACE WAS SHENKIN

LUCY. *Is then his Fate decreed, Sir?*
Such a Man can I think of quitting?

The Beggar's Opera

When first we met, so moves me yet,
O see how my Heart is splitting!

Lock. Look ye, Lucy—There is no saving him. So, I think you must ev'n do like other Widows. Buy your self Weeds, and be cheerful.

AIR XIV

You'll think e'er many Days ensue
This Sentence not severe;

I hang your Husband, Child, 'tis true,
But with him hang your Care.
Twang dang dillo dee.

Like a good Wife, go moan over your dying Husband. That, Child, is your Duty. Consider, Girl, you can't have the Man and the Money too—so make yourself as easy as you can, by getting all you can from him.

SCENE XII

LUCY, MACHEATH.

Lucy. Though the Ordinary was out of the way to-day I hope, my Dear, you will upon the first opportunity quiet my Scruples—Oh Sir!—my Father's hard Heart is not to be soften'd, and I am in the utmost Despair.

Mac. But if I could raise a small Sum—would not twenty Guineas, think you, move him? Of all the Arguments in the way of Business, the Perquisite is the most prevailing. Your Father's Perquisites for the Escape of Prisoners must amount to a considerable Sum in the Year. Money well tim'd, and properly apply'd, will do any thing.

AIR XV. LONDON LADIES

If you at an Office solicit your Due,
　　And would not have Matters neglected;
You must quicken the Clerk with the perquisite too,
　　To do what his Duty directed.
Or would you the Frowns of a Lady prevent,
　　She too has this palpable Failing
The Perquisite softens her into Consent;
　　That Reason with all is prevailing.

Lucy. What Love or Money can do shall be done: for all my Comfort depends upon your Safety.

SCENE XIII

LUCY, MACHEATH, POLLY.

Polly. Where is my dear Husband?—Was a Rope ever intended for this Neck!—O let me throw my Arms about it, and throttle thee with Love! Why dost thou turn away from me? 'Tis thy Polly—'tis thy Wife.

Mac. Was ever such an unfortunate Rascal as I am!

Lucy. Was there ever such another Villain!

Polly. O Macheath! was it for this we parted? Taken! Imprison'd! Try'd! Hang'd!—cruel Reflection! I'll stay with thee 'till Death—no Force shall tear thy dear Wife from thee now.— What means my Love? Not one kind Word! not one kind Look! think what thy Polly suffers to see thee in this Condition.

AIR XVI. ALL IN THE DOWNS, &c.

Thus when the Swallow, seeking Prey,
Within the Sash is closely pent,
His Comfort, with bemoaning Lay,

Without sits pining for th' Event.
Her chatt'ring Lovers all around her skim;
She heeds them not (poor Bird!), her Soul's with him.

Mac.   I must disown her. [*Aside.*] The Wench is distracted.

Lucy.   Am I then bilk'd of my Virtue? Can I have no Reparation? Sure Men were born to lye, and Women to believe them! O Villain! Villain!

Polly.   Am I not thy Wife? Thy Neglect of me, thy Aversion to me too severely proves it. Look on me. Tell me, am I not thy Wife?

Lucy.   Perfidious Wretch!

Polly.   Barbarous Husband!

Lucy.   Hadst thou been hang'd five Months ago, I had been happy.

Polly.   And I too—if you had been kind to me 'till Death, it would not have vex'd me. And that's no very unreasonable

Request, (though from a Wife) to a Man who hath not above seven or eight Days to live.

Lucy. Art thou then married to another? Hast thou two Wives, Monster?

Mac. If Women's Tongues can cease for an Answer—hear me.

Lucy. I won't. Flesh and Blood can't bear my Usage.

Polly. Shall I not claim my own? Justice bids me speak.

AIR XVII. HAVE YOU HEARD OF A FROLICKSOME DITTY, &c.

MAC. *How happy could I be with either,*
Were t'other dear Charmer away!
But while you thus teaze me together,
To neither a Word will I say;
But tol de rol, &c.

Polly. Sure, my Dear, there ought to be some Preference shown to a Wife! At least she may claim the Appearance of it. He must be distracted with his Misfortunes, or he could not use me thus!

Lucy. O Villain, Villain! thou hast deceiv'd me—I could even inform against thee with Pleasure. Not a Prude wishes more heartily to have Facts against her intimate Acquaintance, than I now wish to have Facts against thee. I would have her Satisfaction, and they should all out.

AIR XVIII. IRISH TROT

POLLY.   *I'm bubbled.*
LUCY.....*I'm bubbled.*
POLLY.   *Oh how I am troubled!*
LUCY.   *Bambouzled, and bit!*
POLLY.....*My Distresses are doubled.*

LUCY.   *When you come to the Tree,*
Should the Hangman refuse,
These Fingers, with Pleasure,
Could fasten the Noose.
POLLY.   *I'm bubbled, &c.*

Mac. Be pacified, my dear Lucy—This is all a Fetch of Polly's, to make me desperate with you in case I get off. If I am hang'd, she would fain have the Credit of being thought my Widow. Really, Polly, this is no time for a Dispute of this sort; for whenever you are talking of Marriage, I am thinking of Hanging.

Polly.　And hast thou the Heart to persist in disowning me?

Mac.　And hast thou the Heart to persist in persuading me that I am married? Why, Polly, dost thou seek to aggravate my Misfortunes?

Lucy.　Really, Miss Peachum, you but expose yourself. Besides, 'tis barbarous in you to worry a Gentleman in his Circumstances.

AIR XIX

POLLY.　*Cease your Funning;*
Force or Cunning
Never shall my Heart trapan.
All these Sallies
Are but Malice
To seduce my constant Man.
'Tis most certain,

By their flirting
Women oft have Envy shown;
Pleas'd, to ruin
Others, wooing;
Never happy in their own!

Polly.   Decency, Madam, methinks might teach you to behave yourself with some Reserve with the Husband, while his Wife is present.

Mac.   But seriously, Polly, this is carrying the Joke a little too far.

Lucy.   If you are determin'd, Madam, to raise a Disturbance in the Prison, I shall be oblig'd to send for the Turnkey to show you the Door. I am sorry, Madam, you force me to be so ill-bred.

Polly.   Give me leave to tell you, Madam: These forward Airs don't become you in the least, Madam. And my Duty, Madam, obliges me to stay with my Husband, Madam.

AIR XX. GOOD-MORROW, GOSSIP JOAN

LUCY.   *Why how now, Madam Flirt?*
If you thus must chatter;
And are for flinging Dirt,
Let's try for best can spatter;
        Madam Flirt!
POLLY.   *Why how now, saucy Jade;*
Sure the Wench is Tipsy!

How can you see me made   [*To him.*
The Scoff of such a Gipsy?
Saucy Jade!   [*To her.*

SCENE XIV

LUCY, MACHEATH, POLLY, PEACHUM.

Peach.   Where's my Wench? Ah Hussy! Hussy!—Come you home, you Slut; and when your Fellow is hang'd, hang yourself, to make your Family some amends.

Polly.   Dear, dear Father, do not tear me from him—I must speak; I have more to say to him—Oh! twist thy Fetters about me, that he may not haul me from thee!

Peach.   Sure all Women are alike! If ever they commit the Folly, they are sure to commit another by exposing themselves —away—not a Word more—you are my Prisoner now, Hussy.

AIR XXI. IRISH HOWL

POLLY.   *No Power on Earth can e'er divide,*
The Knot that Sacred Love hath ty'd.

When Parents draw against our Mind,
The True-love's Knot they faster bind.
Oh, oh ray, oh Amborah–oh, oh, &c.
[*Holding* MACHEATH, PEACHUM *pulling her.*

SCENE XV

LUCY, MACHEATH.

Mac.   I am naturally compassionate, Wife; so that I could not use the Wench as she deserv'd; which made you at first suspect there was something in what she said.

Lucy.   Indeed, my Dear, I was strangely puzzled.

Mac. If that had been the Case, her Father would never have brought me into this Circumstance. No, Lucy, I had rather dye than be false to thee.

Lucy. How happy am I, if you say this from your Heart! For I love thee so, that I could sooner bear to see thee hang'd than in the Arms of Another.

Mac. But couldst thou bear to see me hang'd?

Lucy. O Macheath, I can never live to see that Day.

Mac. You see, Lucy, in the Account of Love you are in my debt, and you must now be convinc'd that I rather chuse to die than be another's. Make me, if possible, love thee more, and let me owe my Life to thee. If you refuse to assist me, Peachum and your Father will immediately put me beyond all means of Escape.

Lucy. My Father, I know, hath been drinking hard with the Prisoners: and I fancy he is now taking his Nap in his own Room—if I can procure the Keys, shall I go off with thee, my Dear?

Mac. If we are together, 'twill be impossible to lye conceal'd. As soon as the Search begins to be a little cool, I will send to thee. 'Till then my heart is thy Prisoner.

Lucy. Come then, my dear Husband, owe thy life to me —and though you love me not, be grateful. But that Polly runs in my Head strangely.

Mac. A Moment of time may make us unhappy for ever.

AIR XXII. THE LASS OF PATIE'S MILL, &c.

LUCY.   *I like the Fox shall grieve,*
Whose Mate hath left her side,
Whom Hounds, from Morn to Eve,
Chase o'er the Country wide.

Where can my Lover hide?
Where cheat the weary Pack?
If Love be not his Guide,
He never will come back!

ACT III SCENE I

Newgate

LOCKIT, LUCY.

Lock. To be sure, Wench, you must have been aiding and abetting to help him to this Escape.

Lucy. Sir, here hath been Peachum and his Daughter Polly, and to be sure they know the Ways of Newgate as well as if they had been born and bred in the Place all their Lives. Why must all your Suspicion light upon me?

Lock. Lucy, Lucy, I will have none of these shuffling Answers.

Lucy. Well then—If I know any Thing of him I wish I may be burnt!

Lock. Keep your Temper, Lucy, or I shall pronounce you guilty.

Lucy. Keep yours, Sir—I do wish I may be burnt. I do—and what can I say more to convince you?

Lock. Did he tip handsomely? How much did he come down with? Come Hussy, don't cheat your Father; and I shall not be angry with you—perhaps, you have made a better Bargain with him than I could have done. How much, my good Girl?

Lucy. You know, Sir, I am fond of him, and would have given Money to have kept him with me.

Lock. Ah, Lucy! thy Education might have put thee more

upon thy Guard; for a Girl in the Bar of an Alehouse is always besieg'd.

Lucy. Dear Sir, mention not my Education—for 'twas to that I owe my Ruin.

AIR I. IF LOVE'S A SWEET PASSION, &c.

When young at the Bar you first taught me to score,
And bid me be free of my Lips, and no more;
I was kiss'd by the Parson, the Squire, and the Sot.

When the Guest was departed, the Kiss was forgot.
But his Kiss was so sweet, and so closely he prest,
That I languish'd and pin'd till I granted the rest.

If you can forgive me, Sir, I will make a fair Confession, for to be sure he hath been a most barbarous Villain to me.

Lock. And so you have let him escape, Hussy—have you?

Lucy. When a Woman loves, a kind Look, a tender Word can persuade her to do any thing. And I could ask no other Bribe.

Lock. Thou wilt always be a vulgar Slut, Lucy. If you would not be look'd upon as a Fool, you should never do any thing but upon the Foot of Interest. Those that act otherwise are their own Bubbles.

Lucy. But Love, Sir, is a Misfortune that may happen to the most discreet Woman, and in Love we are all Fools alike. Notwithstanding all he swore, I am now fully convinc'd that Polly Peachum is actually his Wife.—Did I let him escape, —Fool that I was!—to go to her? Polly will wheedle herself into his Money, and then Peachum will hang him, and cheat us both.

Lock. So I am to be ruin'd, because forsooth, you must be in Love!—a very pretty Excuse!

Lucy. I could murder that impudent happy Strumpet: I gave him his Life, and that Creature enjoys the Sweets of it. Ungrateful Macheath!

AIR II. SOUTH-SEA BALLAD

My Love is all Madness and Folly,
Alone I lye,
Toss, tumble, and cry,
What a happy Creature is Polly!

Jenny
Diver
and Suky
Tawdry

Was e'er such a Wretch as I!
With Rage I redden like Scarlet,
That my dear inconstant Varlet,
Stark blind to my Charms,
Is lost in the Arms
Of that Jilt, that inveigling Harlot!
Stark blind to my Charms,
Is lost in the Arms
Of that Jilt, that inveigling Harlot!
This, this my Resentment alarms.

Lock. And so, after all this Mischief, I must stay here to be entertain'd with your catterwauling, Mistress Puss!—Out of my sight, wanton Strumpet! you shall fast and fortify yourself into Reason, with now and then a little handsome Discipline to bring you to your Senses.—Go.

SCENE II

LOCKIT.

Peachum then intends to outwit me in this Affair; but I'll be even with him—The Dog is leaky in his Liquor, so I'll ply him that way, get the Secret from him, and turn this Affair to my own Advantage.—Lions, Wolves, and Vultures don't live together in Herds, Droves or Flocks.—Of all Animals of Prey, Man is the only sociable one. Every one of us preys upon his Neighbour, and yet we herd together. Peachum is my Companion, my Friend—according to the Customs of the World, indeed, he may quote thousands of Precedents for cheating me. And shall not I make use of the Privilege of Friendship to make him a Return?

AIR III. PACKINGTON'S POUND

Thus Gamesters united in Friendship are found,
Though they know that their Industry all is a Cheat;
They flock to their Prey at the Dice-Box's Sound,

And join to promote one another's Deceit.
But if by mishap
They fail of a Chap,
To keep in their Hands, they each other entrap.
Like Pikes, lank with Hunger, who miss of their Ends,
They bite their Companions, and prey on their Friends.

Now, Peachum, you and I, like honest Tradesmen, are to have a fair Tryal which of us two can over-reach the other. Lucy.

Enter LUCY.

Are there any of Peachum's People now in the House?

Lucy.   Filch, Sir, is drinking a Quartern of Strong-Waters in the next Room with Black Moll.

Lock.   Bid him come to me.

SCENE III

LOCKIT, FILCH.

Lock.   Why, Boy, thou lookest as if thou wert half starv'd; like a shotten Herring.

Filch.   One had need have the Constitution of a Horse to go through the Business. Since the favourite Child-getter was disabled by a Mis-hap, I have pick'd up a little Money by helping the Ladies to a Pregnancy against their being call'd down to Sentence. But if a Man cannot get an honest Livelihood any easier way, I am sure 'tis what I can't undertake for another Session.

Lock. Truly, if that great Man should tip off, 'twould be an irreparable Loss. The Vigour and Prowess of a Knight Errant never sav'd half the Ladies in Distress that he hath done. But, Boy, can'st thou tell me where thy Master is to be found?

Filch. At his Lock, Sir, at the Crooked Billet.

Lock. Very well. I have nothing more with you. [*Exit* FILCH.] I'll go to him there, for I have many important Affairs to settle with him; and in the way of those Transactions, I'll artfully get into his Secret, so that Macheath shall not remain a Day longer out of my Clutches.

SCENE IV

A Gaming-House

MACHEATH *in a fine tarnish'd Coat*, BEN BUDGE, MATT OF THE MINT.

Mac. I am sorry, Gentlemen, the Road was so barren of Money. When my Friends are in Difficulties, I am always glad that my Fortune can be serviceable to them. [*Gives them Money.*] You see, Gentlemen, I am not a mere Court Friend, who professes every thing and will do nothing.

AIR IV. LILLIBULLERO

The Modes of the Court so common are grown,
That a true Friend can hardly be met;
Friendship for Interest is but a Loan,

Which they let out for what they can get.
'Tis true, you find
Some Friends so kind,
Who will give you good Counsel themselves to defend.
In sorrowful Ditty,
They promise, they pity,
But shift you for Money, from Friend to Friend.

But we, Gentlemen, have still Honour enough to break through the Corruptions of the World. And while I can serve you, you may command me.

Ben. It grieves my Heart that so generous a Man should be involv'd in such Difficulties, as oblige him to live with such ill Company, and herd with Gamesters.

Matt. See the Partiality of Mankind! One Man may steal a Horse, better than another look over a Hedge. Of all Mechanics, of all servile Handy-crafts-men, a Gamester is the vilest. But yet, as many of the Quality are of the Profession, he is admitted amongst the politest Company. I wonder we are not more respected.

Mach. There will be deep Play to-night at Marybone, and consequently Money may be pick'd up upon the Road. Meet me there, and I'll give you the Hint who is worth Setting.

Matt. The Fellow with a brown Coat with a narrow Gold Binding, I am told, is never without Money.

Mach. What do you mean, Matt? Sure you will not think of meddling with him! He's a good honest kind of a Fellow, and one of us.

Ben. To be sure, Sir, we will put our selves under your Direction.

Mach. Have an Eye upon the Money-Lenders. A Rouleau or two would prove a pretty sort of an Expedition. I hate Extortion.

Matt. Those Rouleaus are very pretty Things. I hate your Bank Bills; there is such a Hazard in putting them off.

Mach. There is a certain Man of Distinction, who in his Time hath nick'd me out of a great deal of the Ready. He is in my Cash, Ben; I'll point him out to you this Evening, and you shall draw upon him for the Debt. The Company are met; I hear the Dice-box in the other Room. So, Gentlemen, your Servant. You'll meet me at Marybone.

SCENE V

PEACHUM'S *Lock*

A Table with Wine, Brandy, Pipes and Tobacco.
PEACHUM, LOCKIT.

Lock. The Coronation Account, Brother Peachum, is of so intricate a Nature, that I believe it will never be settled.

Peach. It consists indeed of a great Variety of Articles. It was worth to our People, in Fees of different Kinds, above ten Instalments. This is part of the Account, Brother, that lies open before us.

Lock. A Lady's Tail of rich Brocade—that, I see, is dispos'd of.

Peach. To Mrs. Diana Trapes, the Tally-woman, and she will make a good Hand on't in Shoes and Slippers, to trick out young Ladies, upon their going into Keeping.

Lock. But I don't see any Article of the Jewels.

Peach. Those are so well known, that they must be sent abroad. You'll find them enter'd under the Article of Exportation. As for the Snuff-Boxes, Watches, Swords, &c., I thought it best to enter them under their several Heads.

Lock. Seven-and-twenty Women's Pockets compleat; with the several things therein contain'd; all Seal'd, Number'd, and enter'd.

Peach. But, Brother, it is impossible for us now to enter upon this Affair. We should have the whole Day before us.

Besides, the Account of the last Half Year's Plate is in a Book by it self, which lies at the other Office.

Lock. Bring us then more Liquor. To-day shall be for Pleasure, To-morrow for Business. Ah, Brother, those Daughters of ours are two flippery Hussies. Keep a watchful Eye upon Polly, and Macheath in a Day or two shall be our own again.

AIR V. DOWN IN THE NORTH COUNTRY, &c.

> LOCK. *What Gudgeons are we Men!*
> *Ev'ry Woman's easy Prey.*
> *Though we have felt the Hook, again*
> *We bite and they betray.*

> *The Bird that hath been trapt,*
> *When he hears his calling Mate,*
> *To her he flies, again he's clapt*
> *Within the wiry Grate.*

Peach. But what signifies catching the Bird, if your Daughter Lucy will set open the Door of the Cage?

Lock. If Men were answerable for the Follies and Frailties

Mrs.
Trapes

of their Wives and Daughters, no Friends could keep a good Correspondence together for two Days. This is unkind of you, Brother; for among good Friends, what they say or do goes for nothing.

Enter a SERVANT.

Serv.   Sir, here's Mrs. Diana Trapes wants to speak with you.

Peach.   Shall we admit her, Brother Lockit?

Lock.   By all means—she's a good Customer, and a fine-spoken Woman, and a Woman who drinks and talks so freely, will enliven the Conversation.

Peach.   Desire her to walk in.   [*Exit* SERVANT.

SCENE VI

PEACHUM, LOCKIT, MRS. TRAPES.

Peach.   Dear Mrs. Dye, your Servant. One may know by your Kiss, that your Ginn is excellent.

Trapes.   I was always very curious in my Liquors.

Lock.   There is no perfum'd Breath like it. I have been long acquainted with the Flavour of those Lips—han't I, Mrs. Dye?

Trapes.   Fill it up. I take as large Draughts of Liquor, as I did of Love. I hate a Flincher in either.

AIR VI. A SHEPHERD KEPT SHEEP, &c.

In the Days of my Youth I could bill like a Dove, fa, la, la, &c.
Like a Sparrow at all times was ready for Love, fa, la, la, &c.
The Life of all Mortals in Kissing should pass,
Lip to Lip while we're young—then the Lip to the Glass, fa, &c.

But now, Mr. Peachum, to our Business. If you have Blacks of any kind brought in of late, Mantoes, Velvet Scarfs, Petticoats, let it be what it will—I am your Chap; for all my Ladies are very fond of Mourning.

Peach. Why, look ye, Mrs. Dye—you deal so hard with us, that we can afford to give the Gentlemen who venture their Lives for the Goods, little or nothing.

Trapes. The hard Times oblige me to go very near in my Dealing. To be sure, of late Years I have been a great Sufferer by the Parliament. Three thousand Pounds would hardly make me amends. The Act for destroying the Mint, was a severe Cut upon our Business. 'Till then, if a Customer stept out of the way we knew where to have her. No doubt you know Mrs. Coaxer—there's a Wench now—'till to-day—with a good Suit of Cloaths of mine upon her Back, and I could never set Eyes upon her for three Months together. Since the Act too against Imprisonment for small Sums, my Loss there too hath been very considerable, and it must be so, when a Lady can borrow a handsome Petticoat, or a clean Gown, and I not have the least Hank upon her! And, o' my conscience, now-a-days most Ladies take a Delight in cheating, when they can do it with Safety.

Peach.   Madam, you had a handsome Gold Watch of us t'other Day for seven Guineas. Considering we must have our Profit—to a Gentleman upon the Road, a Gold Watch will be scarce worth the taking.

Trap.   Consider, Mr. Peachum, that Watch was remarkable, and not of very safe sale. If you have any black Velvet Scarfs—they are a handsome Winter-wear, and take with most Gentlemen who deal with my Customers. 'Tis I that put the Ladies upon a good Foot. 'Tis not Youth or Beauty that fixes their Price. The Gentlemen always pay according to their Dress, from half a Crown to two Guineas; and yet those Hussies make nothing of bilking of me. Then, too, allowing for Accidents—I have eleven fine Customers now down under the Surgeon's Hands; what with Fees and other Expences, there are great Goings-out, and no Comings-in, and not a

Farthing to pay for at least a Month's cloathing. We run great Risques—great Risques indeed.

Peach. As I remember, you said something just now of Mrs. Coaxer.

Trap. Yes, Sir. To be sure I stript her of a Suit of my own Cloaths about two hours ago; and have left her as she should be, in her Shift, with a Lover of hers at my House. She call'd him up Stairs, as he was going to Marybone in a Hackney Coach. And I hope, for her own sake and mine, she will persuade the Captain to redeem her, for the Captain is very generous to the Ladies.

Lock. What Captain?

Trap. He thought I did not know him—an intimate Acquaintance of yours, Mr. Peachum. Only Captain Macheath —as fine as a Lord.

Peach. To-morrow, dear Mrs. Dye, you shall set your own Price upon any of the Goods you like. We have at least half a dozen Velvet Scarfs, and all at your service. Will you give me leave to make you a Present of this Suit of Night-Cloaths for your own wearing? But are you sure it is Captain Macheath?

Trap. Though he thinks I have forgot him, no Body knows him better. I have taken a great deal of the Captain's Money in my Time at second-hand, for he always lov'd to have his Ladies well drest.

Peach. Mr. Lockit and I have a little business with the Captain;—you understand me—and we will satisfye you for Mrs. Coaxer's Debt.

Lock. Depend upon it, we will deal like Men of Honour.

Trap. I don't enquire after your Affairs, so whatever happens, I wash my Hands on't. It hath always been my Maxim, that one Friend should assist another. But if you please, I'll take one of the Scarfs home with me. 'Tis always good to have something in Hand.

SCENE VII

Newgate

LUCY, FILCH.

Lucy. Jealousy, Rage, Love and Fear are at once tearing me to pieces. How I am weather-beaten and shatter'd with distresses!

AIR VII. ONE EVENING, HAVING LOST MY WAY, &c.

I'm like a Skiff on the Ocean tost,
Now high, now low, with each Billow born,
With her Rudder broke, and her Anchor lost,
Deserted and all forlorn.
While thus I lye rolling and tossing all Night,
That Polly lyes sporting on Seas of Delight!
Revenge, Revenge, Revenge,
Shall appease my restless Sprite.

I have the Rats-bane ready. I run no Risque; for I can lay her Death upon the Ginn, and so many dye of that naturally that I shall never be call'd in Question. But say I were to be hang'd —I never could be hang'd for any thing that would give me greater Comfort, than the poysoning that Slut.

Enter FILCH.

Filch. Madam, here's our Miss Polly come to wait upon you.
Lucy. Show her in.

SCENE VIII

LUCY, POLLY.

Lucy. Dear Madam, your Servant. I hope you will pardon my Passion, when I was so happy as to see you last. I was so over-run with the Spleen, that I was perfectly out of my self. And really when one hath the Spleen, every thing is to be excus'd by a Friend.

AIR VIII. NOW ROGER, I'LL TELL THEE,
BECAUSE THOU'RT MY SON

When a Wife's in her Pout
(As she's sometimes, no doubt;)
The good Husband as meek as a Lamb,

Her Vapours to still,
First grants her her Will,
And the quieting Draught is a Dram.
Poor Man! And the quieting Draught is a Dram.

I wish all our Quarrels might have so comfortable a Reconciliation.

Polly. I have no Excuse for my own Behaviour, Madam, but my Misfortunes. And really, Madam, I suffer too upon your Account.

Lucy. But, Miss Polly—in the way of Friendship, will you give me leave to propose a Glass of Cordial to you?

Polly. Strong-Waters are apt to give me the Head-ache—I hope, Madam, you will excuse me.

Lucy. Not the greatest Lady in the Land could have better in her Closet, for her own private drinking.—You seem mighty low in Spirits, my Dear.

Polly. I am sorry, Madam, my Health will not allow me to accept of your Offer. I should not have left you in the rude Manner I did when we met last, Madam, had not my Papa haul'd me away so unexpectedly—I was indeed somewhat provok'd, and perhaps might use some Expressions that were disrespectful. But really, Madam, the Captain treated me with so much Contempt and Cruelty, that I deserv'd your Pity, rather than your Resentment.

Lucy. But since his Escape, no doubt all Matters are made up again. Ah Polly! Polly! 'tis I am the unhappy Wife; and he loves you as if you were only his Mistress.

Polly. Sure, Madam, you cannot think me so happy as to be the Object of your Jealousy. A Man is always afraid of a Woman who loves him too well—so that I must expect to be neglected and avoided.

Lucy. Then our Cases, my dear Polly, are exactly alike. Both of us indeed have been too fond.

AIR IX. O BESSY BELL

POLLY. *A Curse attends that Woman's Love,*
  Who always would be pleasing.
LUCY. *The Pertness of the billing Dove,*
  Like tickling, is but teazing.

Lucy
Lockit

POLLY.   *What then in Love can Woman do?*
LUCY.   *If we grow fond, they shun us.*
POLLY.   *And when we fly them, they pursue.*
LUCY.   *But leave us when they've won us.*

Lucy.   Love is so very whimsical in both Sexes, that it is impossible to be lasting. But my Heart is particular, and contradicts my own Observation.

Polly.   But really, Mistress Lucy, by his last Behaviour, I think I ought to envy you. When I was forc'd from him, he did not shew the least Tenderness. But perhaps, he hath a Heart not capable of it.

AIR X. WOULD FATE TO ME BELINDA GIVE—

Among the Men, Coquets we find,
Who Court by turns all Woman-kind;

And we grant all their Hearts desir'd,
When they are flatter'd, and admir'd.

The Coquets of both Sexes are Self-lovers, and that is a Love no other whatever can dispossess. I fear, my dear Lucy, our Husband is one of those.

Lucy. Away with these melancholy Reflections—indeed, my dear Polly, we are both of us a Cup too low. Let me prevail upon you to accept of my Offer.

AIR XI. COME, SWEET LASS, &c.

Come, sweet Lass,
Let's banish Sorrow
'Till To-morrow;
Come, sweet Lass,
Let's take a chirping Glass.
Wine can clear

The Vapours of Despair;
And make us light as Air;
Then drink, and banish Care.

I can't bear, Child, to see you in such low Spirits.—And I must persuade you to what I know will do you good.—I shall now soon be even with the hypocritical Strumpet.　　　　　　*[Aside.*

SCENE IX

POLLY.

All this wheedling of Lucy cannot be for nothing. At this time too! when I know she hates me! The Dissembling of a Woman is always the Fore-runner of Mischief. By pouring Strong-Waters down my Throat, she thinks to pump some secrets out of me. I'll be upon my Guard, and won't taste a Drop of her Liquor, I'm resolv'd.

SCENE X

LUCY, *with Strong-Waters.* POLLY.

Lucy. Come, Miss Polly.

Polly. Indeed, Child, you have given yourself trouble to no purpose. You must, my Dear, excuse me.

Lucy. Really, Miss Polly, you are so squeamishly affected about taking a Cup of Strong-Waters as a Lady before Company. I vow, Polly, I shall take it monstrously ill if you refuse me. Brandy and Men (though Women love them never so well) are always taken by us with some Reluctance—unless 'tis in private.

Polly. I protest, Madam, it goes against me.—What do I see! Macheath again in Custody!—Now every glimm'ring of Happiness is lost.

[*Drops the Glass of Liquor on the Ground.*

Lucy. Since things are thus, I'm glad the Wench hath escap'd: for by this Event, 'tis plain, she was not happy enough to deserve to be poyson'd. [*Aside.*

SCENE XI

LOCKIT, MACHEATH, PEACHUM, LUCY, POLLY.

Lock. Set your Heart to rest, Captain. You have neither the Chance of Love or Money for another Escape, for you are order'd to be call'd down upon your Tryal immediately.

Peach. Away, Hussies! This is not a time for a Man to be hamper'd with his Wives. You see, the Gentleman is in Chains already.

Lucy. O Husband, Husband, my heart long'd to see thee; but to see thee thus distracts me!

Polly. Will not my dear Husband look upon his Polly? Why hadst thou not flown to me for Protection? with me thou hadst been safe.

AIR XII. THE LAST TIME I WENT O'ER THE MOOR

POLLY. *Hither, dear Husband, turn your Eyes.*
LUCY. *Bestow one Glance to cheer me.*
POLLY. *Think with that Look, thy Polly dyes.*
LUCY. *O shun me not—but hear me.*
POLLY. *'Tis Polly sues.*
LUCY.... *'Tis Lucy speaks.*
POLLY. *Is this true Love requited?*

LUCY.   *My Heart is bursting.*
POLLY.... *Mine too breaks.*
LUCY.   *Must I*
POLLY.... *Must I be slighted?*

Mach.   What would you have me say, Ladies?—You see, this Affair will soon be at an end, without my disobliging either of you.

Peach.   But the settling this Point, Captain, might prevent a Law-suit between your two Widows.

AIR XIII.   TOM TINKER'S MY TRUE LOVE

MACH.   *Which way shall I turn me? How can I decide?*
Wives, the Day of our Death, are as fond as a Bride.
One Wife is too much for most Husbands to bear,

But two at a time there's no Mortal can bear.
This way, and that way, and which way I will,
What would comfort the one, t'other Wife would take ill.

Polly. But if his own Misfortunes have made him insensible to mine—a Father sure will be more compassionate.—Dear, dear Sir, sink the material Evidence, and bring him off at his Tryal—Polly upon her Knees begs it of you.

AIR XIV. I AM A POOR SHEPHERD UNDONE

When my Hero in Court appears,
And stands arraign'd for his Life;
Then think of poor Polly's Tears;
For Ah! Poor Polly's his Wife.
Like the Sailor he holds up his Hand,

Distrest on the dashing Wave.
To die a dry Death at Land,
Is as bad as a watry Grave.
And alas, poor Polly!
Alack, and well-a-day!
Before I was in Love,
Oh! every Month was May.

Lucy. If Peachum's Heart is harden'd, sure you, Sir, will have more Compassion on a Daughter. I know the Evidence is in your Power. How then can you be a Tyrant to me?

[Kneeling.

AIR XV. IANTH THE LOVELY, &c.

When he holds up his Hand arraign'd for his Life,
O think of your Daughter, and think I'm his Wife!

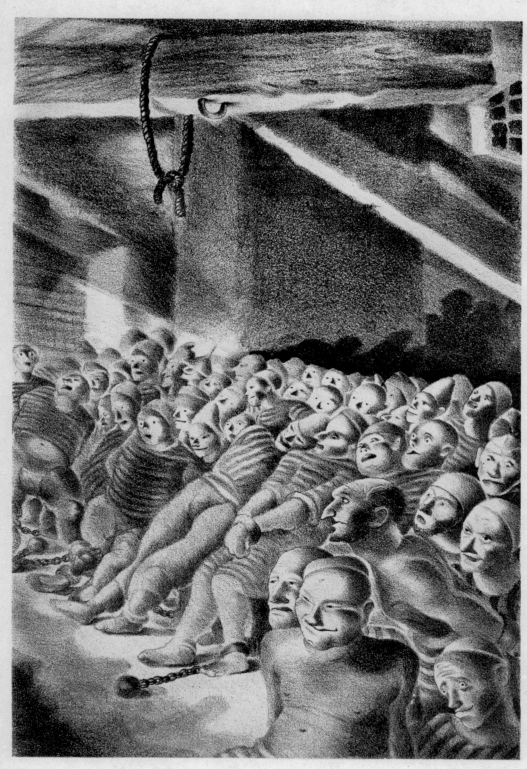

Dance
of the
Prisoners

What are Cannons, or Bombs, or clashing of Swords?
For Death is more certain by Witnesses' Words.
Then nail up their Lips; that dread Thunder allay;
And each Month of my Life will hereafter be May.

Lock.   Macheath's time is come, Lucy. We know our own Affairs, therefore let us have no more Whimpering or Whining.

Peach.   Set your Heart at rest, Polly. Your Husband is to dye to-day. Therefore, if you are not already provided, 'tis high time to look about for another. There's Comfort for you, you Slut.

Lock.   We are ready, Sir, to conduct you to the Old Bailey.

AIR XVI. BONNY DUNDEE

MACH.   *The Charge is prepar'd; The Lawyers are met,*
                The Judges all rang'd (a terrible Show!)
                I go, undismay'd.—For Death is a Debt,
                A Debt on demand.—So, take what I owe.
                Then farewell, my Love—dear Charmers, adieu.
                Contented I die—'tis the better for you.
                Here ends all Dispute the rest of our Lives.
                For this way at once I please all my Wives.

Now, Gentlemen, I am ready to attend you.

SCENE XII

LUCY, POLLY, FILCH.

Polly.   Follow them, Filch, to the Court. And when the Tryal is over, bring me a particular Account of his Behaviour, and of every thing that happen'd.—You'll find me here with Miss Lucy. [*Exit* FILCH.] But why is all this Musick?

Lucy.   The Prisoners, whose Tryals are put off till next Session, are diverting themselves.

Polly.   Sure there is nothing so charming as Musick! I'm fond of it to distraction!—But alas!—now, all Mirth seems an Insult upon my Affliction. Let us retire, my dear Lucy, and indulge our Sorrows. The noisy Crew, you see, are coming upon us.   [*Exeunt.*
                           [*A Dance of Prisoners in Chains, &c.*

Act III Scene XIII

SCENE XIII

The Condemn'd Hold

MACHEATH, *in a melancholy Posture.*

AIR XVII. HAPPY GROVES

O cruel, cruel, cruel Case!
Must I suffer this Disgrace?

AIR XVIII. OF ALL THE GIRLS THAT ARE SO SMART

Of all the Friends in time of Grief,
When threatening Death looks grimmer,
*   Not one so sure can bring Relief,*
*   As this best Friend, a Brimmer.*   [*Drinks.*

AIR XIX. BRITONS

Since I must swing,—I scorn, I scorn to wince or whine.   [*Rises.*

The Beggar's Opera

AIR XX. CHEVY CHASE

But now again my Spirits sink;
I'll raise them high with Wine.   *[Drinks a Glass of Wine.*

AIR XXI. TO OLD SIR SIMON THE KING

But Valour the stronger grows,
The stronger Liquor we're drinking.
And how can we feel our Woes,
When we've lost the Trouble of Thinking?   *[Drinks.*

AIR XXII. JOY TO GREAT CAESAR

If thus—a Man can die

          [Pours out a Bumper of Brandy.

Act III Scene XIII

AIR XXIII. THERE WAS AN OLD WOMAN

So I drink off this Bumper—and now I can stand the Test.
And my Comrades shall see, that I die as brave as the Best. [Drinks.

AIR XXIV. DID YOU EVER HEAR OF A GALLANT SAILOR

But can I leave my pretty Hussies,
Without one Tear, or tender Sigh?

AIR XXV. WHY ARE MINE EYES STILL FLOWING

Their Eyes, their Lips, their Busses
Recall my Love. Ah, must I die!

The Beggar's Opera

AIR XXVI. GREEN SLEEVES

Since Laws were made for ev'ry Degree,
To curb Vice in others, as well as me,
I wonder we han't better Company,
Upon Tyburn Tree!

But Gold from Law can take out the Sting;
And if rich Men like us were to swing,
'Twou'd thin the Land, such Numbers to string
Upon Tyburn Tree!

Jailer.   Some Friends of yours, Captain, desire to be admitted.—I leave you together.

SCENE XIV

MACHEATH, BEN BUDGE, MATT OF THE MINT.

Mach.   For my having broke Prison, you see, Gentlemen, I am order'd immediate Execution. The Sheriff's Officers, I believe, are now at the Door. That Jemmy Twitcher should peach me, I own surpriz'd me! 'Tis a plain Proof that the World is all alike, and that even our Gang can no more trust one another than other People. Therefore I beg you, Gentlemen, look well to yourselves, for in all probability you may live some Months longer.

Matt.   We are heartily sorry, Captain, for your Misfortune. But 'tis what we must all come to.

Mach.   Peachum and Lockit, you know, are infamous Scoundrels. Their Lives are as much in your Power, as yours are in theirs. Remember your dying Friend! 'Tis my last Request. Bring those Villains to the Gallows before you, and I am satisfied.

Matt.   We'll do't.

Jailor.   Miss Polly and Miss Lucy intreat a Word with you.

Mach.   Gentlemen, Adieu.

SCENE XV

LUCY, MACHEATH, POLLY.

Mach.   My dear Lucy—my dear Polly—whatsoever hath past between us is now at an end. If you are fond of marrying again, the best Advice I can give you, is to Ship yourselves off for the West-Indies, where you'll have a fair chance of getting a Husband a-piece; or by good Luck, two or three, as you like best.

Polly. How can I support this Sight!

Lucy. There is nothing moves one so much as a great Man in Distress.

AIR XXVII. ALL YOU THAT MUST TAKE A LEAP, &c.

LUCY.   *Would I might be hang'd!*

POLLY.... *And I would so too!*

LUCY.   *To be hang'd with you.*

POLLY.... *My Dear, with you.*

MACH.   *O Leave me to Thought! I fear! I doubt!*
I tremble! I droop!—See, my Courage is out.

> [*Turns up the empty Bottle.*

POLLY.   *No token of Love?*

MACH.... *See, my Courage is out.*

> [*Turns up the empty Pot.*

LUCY.   *No token of Love?*

POLLY.... *Adieu.*

LUCY.... *Farewell.*

MACH.   *But hark! I hear the Toll of the Bell.*

CHORUS.   *Tol de rol lol, &c.*

Jailor.   Four Women more, Captain, with a Child a-piece!
See, here they come.

> *Enter* WOMEN *and* CHILDREN.

Mach.   What—four Wives more!—This is too much. Here
—tell the Sheriff's Officers I am ready.

> [*Exit* MACHEATH, *guarded.*

SCENE XVI

To them, Enter PLAYER *and* BEGGAR.

Play.   But, honest Friend, I hope you don't intend that
Macheath shall be really executed.

Beg. Most certainly, Sir.—To make the Piece perfect, I was for doing strict poetical Justice. Macheath is to be hang'd; and for the other Personages of the Drama, the Audience must have suppos'd they were all either hang'd or transported.

Play. Why then, Friend, this is a down-right deep Tragedy. The Catastrophe is manifestly wrong, for an Opera must end happily.

Beg. Your Objection, Sir, is very just; and is easily remov'd. For you must allow that in this kind of Drama, 'tis no matter how absurdly things are brought about.—So—you Rabble there—run and cry a Reprieve—let the Prisoner be brought back to his Wives in Triumph.

Play. All this we must do, to comply with the Taste of the Town.

Beg. Through the whole Piece you may observe such a similitude of Manners in high and low Life, that it is difficult to determine whether (in the fashionable Vices) the fine Gentlemen imitate the Gentlemen of the Road, or the Gentlemen of the Road the fine Gentlemen. Had the Play remain'd as I at first intended, it would have carried a most excellent Moral. 'Twould have shown that the lower Sort of People have their Vices in a degree as well as the Rich, and that they are punish'd for them.

SCENE XVII

To them, MACHEATH *with* RABBLE, *&c.*

Mach.   So, it seems, I am not left to my Choice, but must have a Wife at last.—Look ye, my Dears, we will have no Controversie now. Let us give this Day to Mirth, and I am sure she who thinks herself my Wife will testifie her Joy by a Dance.

All.   Come, a Dance—a Dance.

Mach.   Ladies, I hope you will give me leave to present a Partner to each of you. And (if I may without Offence) for this time, I take Polly for mine. And for Life, you Slut—for we were really marry'd. As for the rest—but at present keep your own Secret.   [*To* POLLY.

A DANCE

AIR XXVIII. LUMPS OF PUDDING, &c.

Thus I stand like the Turk, *with his Doxies around;*
From all Sides their Glances his Passion confound;
For black, brown, and fair, his Inconstancy burns,
And the different Beauties subdue him by turns:
Each calls forth her Charms, to provoke his Desires:
Though willing to all, with but one he retires.
But think of this Maxim, and put off your Sorrow,
The Wretch of To-day, may be happy To-morrow.
CHORUS.   *But think of this Maxim, &c.*

The Beggar's Opera

Act III Scene XVII